STANDING ON THE SHOULDERS OF GIANTS: From Father to Dad

Valuing Men for Their Uniqueness as Individuals and as Dads
by Answering Frequently Asked Questions

By
Owen Connolly
Counsellor and Family Therapist

Published by Nurture Press
140 Meadow Grove, Dundrum
Dublin 16, Ireland

Telephone +353 (01) 2963795
for orders and general enquiries

Visit our homepage:
www.nurture.ie <http://www.nurture.ie/>

ISBN 0-9534731-12-0

Project managed by Deirdre Clare

dedication & special thanks

Dedicated to my beautiful grandchildren
– Skye, Soul, Ian, Jai, Ace, and Elle.

Very special thanks to my patient and loving wife Claire.

Special thanks to my sons David and Kevin and my daughters-in-law Lea and Allison, my father Liam and my mother Lil.

For encouragement and inspiration and for introducing me to the principles of intimacy, special thanks are due to Dr. David and Teresa Ferguson of Intimate Life Ministries in Austin, Texas.

Special thanks to Brian Cullen, whose encouragement and support assisted in the production of this book.

For invaluable help with preparing the manuscript, special thanks are due to David Clare.

Thanks also readers Ruth Yoder, Peter Connors, John Broderick, Brian Gogan, and Barry Casey.

Cover design by Lea Petmezas.

table of contents

If I have seen further, it is because I have stood on the Shoulders of Giants.

Sir Isaac Newton

introduction

This is the most confused time in history for men. For centuries, men took a position of authority in the home and in the world. Over the past hundred years, however, women have risen to a place of equality by realising how valuable they are and by using their unique gifts to make the world a better place. One of the results of this is that men no longer understand their role in society. They feel lost because they are no longer in charge and because they feel bad about the ways in which they misused the authority that they had. It is time for men to do what the women did – to examine their unique gifts and to use those gifts to enrich the lives of their families and the society around them. At the moment, men don't understand themselves or realise how valuable they are. Go into any shop and you'll find racks and racks of magazines that say what women need and what they think and how brilliant they are, but if you go looking at the shelves for anything to do with men, you find nothing that deals with them personally – just car magazines, DIY magazines, sports magazines, and magazines designed to titillate, none of which promote a man's value or worth. In this book, by answering some frequently asked questions about being a dad, I hope to encourage men to look at themselves and to understand their natural gifts. These gifts include, among others, leadership, decision-making, and the ability to "put the shoulder to the wheel." Many men feel these particular gifts are unacceptable to the women of today's world, but I hope to show that women still look for these gifts in committed relationships and that men must accept and use all their gifts in order to bless their families and to make this world a better place. I want each man to see the considerable contribution he has to make to his children, and I want to encourage each man to pass on the qualities and values that will help his children survive whatever's thrown at them. After all, it was by our ancestors using their gifts that we have been able to survive as a species in the first place!

SECTION ONE

men and women

The work that I do with regard to personal development is founded mostly on understanding how we're designed and how that design works. For instance, our brain, which is approximately 2 percent of our mass, uses about 25 percent of our energy. There must be a very good reason for that. There must also be a very good reason for the fact that humans are stubborn and persistent when faced with obstacles. And there is – survival. The reason we humans have survived until today is because there are mechanisms placed within us that were designed very specifically for our survival. For instance, we all have a two-tier information highway or two-way tracking system. If we have information coming at us that is threatening, we have mechanisms within ourselves to sense the threat and act defensively against it. If we don't have something threatening coming at us, we have mechanisms that encourages us to wonder and ponder and reflect. These mechanisms help us assess our body and its surroundings and they need to be understood. When a child is needy, its desire to seek out help and input is an instinct for survival and you have instincts that prompt you to help that child. You are, in fact, predisposed to help encourage their growth and continued development. As humans, we want to survive, and therefore we will interact with certain mechanisms within us that have already proven to be successful in helping us. We are the product of those who have survived before us. Going in to the future, we will continue to do what we must to survive, and to assist the survival of the next generation.

Let us now consider some of the most frequently asked questions about men and women and a man's role in his family and the world…

1) In your opinion, are there fundamental differences between men and women and how do they affect the way we parent?

Men and women are different by design. Women are designed to be more focused on security, while men are, in general, more focused on action. As an example of this difference, let us consider a couple that are about to go away on holiday. The man is standing at the door next to his partner, and, being linear or "single-object focused" in his thinking, he's anxious to get in the car and get on the road. He's more likely to be focused on the journey and nothing else. The woman, on the other hand, is better at multi-tasking due to being lateral or "multi-object focused" in her thought processes, and she's thinking about a whole myriad of things. She might ask her partner if he wouldn't mind getting something from the kitchen. He's a bit confused, and doesn't understand why he should get it instead of her. He sees her standing at the door and he doesn't realise she's actually doing many different jobs in her head – checking that all the lights are set on timers and that the water's turned off and that the post is taken care of. She's actually working and the man doesn't realise that, because she's multi-object focused and he's single-object focused at that time. And that can cause problems between them, because they don't realise that their mindsets are different. She's thinking, "What if I don't turn that off? What happens if I don't inform the postman? Etc." She, as a woman, has a need for security and an insecure feeling is prompting this whole investigative process. And that's an essential part of her make-up because she's always looking for the strongest branch on which to build her nest, and she's always going to make sure that her children and home are safe. She's much more conscious of that than most men would be. On the other hand, the man is thinking about the travel arrangements, such as the time of departure and the time of arrival, and these times are sacred to most men. This design in a man is, of course, a very good thing – it's part of men's pioneering excitement over getting to new territory, and working out the journey is an essential part of his internal map-making and decision-making processes.

Another big area of difference between men and women is that, in general, men tend to be more task-focused, so that when a woman speaks to a man about her feelings or emotions, he's at a disadvantage because he's thinking "What does she want me to do?" or "How can I solve this problem?" But she only wants to be heard and understood. Children are a bit like that, too, so it's important that when a father is listening to his wife or young children, he actually listens to the feelings that are being expressed and doesn't rush to provide answers or advice. After he's examined their feelings and really heard what they're saying and sympathised and empathised and assured them that he understands, then – maybe! – he can give advice, acting out his manly way.

A third area of difference is decision-making. The design in the man usually pushes him more towards leadership and "getting things done" and to focus on the fact rather than the feeling. As a result, his decision-making process is usually much faster and less emotionally governed. The friction comes about when the emotional content of the conversation between a man and a woman is not heard and acknowledged, as he rushes to make decisions. Men shouldn't be ashamed of this ability to make tough decisions quickly. Since the beginning of time, man's role as protector has meant that he must possess the ability to act very quickly and to make decisions without emotion. When a man asks for something to be done, he often has an expectation that it should be done right away without question, because, to the person he is protecting, it could mean the difference between life and death. This old survival mechanism often manifests itself today when a father asks his child to carry out some chore in the home. Dad is less tolerant than Mum when the task is not done right away.

Another area of difference is how men and women mind the children. The multi-tasking side of the woman can make the children feel that Mum is not listening. She's not giving eye contact as she does a million and one jobs, and it's quite common for children to want eye contact in order to believe that there is some level of communication between them and their parent. If a woman is multi-tasking, she can be doing many tasks and still be listening – she can be painting the house or ironing the clothes or preparing the family accounts and still be hearing what the children are saying. She needs to either help them understand that she hears through empathetic listening (repeating what they're saying back to them) or, if necessary, take the time to make eye contact. By contrast, many times when the father takes over the parenting role, the children can feel like prisoners, because when the father wants to do anything, he insists that the children sit still and stay where they are till he gets back. And that isn't that the way a mother would typically treat a child. Her ability to hear what's going on around the house and still focus on a task gives her the freedom to let the children move about and do their own thing. She has a sense of their presence around her and can cope with them being out of sight, whereas the man is unlikely to be able to deal with the out-of-sight child. He needs to know where that child is and that he or she is not going to move till he gets back. All this becomes evident when you see the men caring for their children on a Saturday afternoon in a park. "Don't move – stay on this bench – I want you to be there when I get back." A man does this because his valuable design as protector tells him that if the children are out of his sight, they may be unsafe. But a father must realise when his children are starting to feel trapped and learn to be more relaxed as they move around. As men and women, there are many behaviours which we have to learn in order to overcome the survival-instinct messages which our feelings send to us. We have to ignore these feelings and learn these more moderate behaviours in order to accommodate the needs of the present day. (For example, without these learned behaviours, our innate emotional response would have us assault our neighbour if we found him or her threatening!)

Although men in general are more single-focused when minding the children, they are not nearly as overly concerned for the safety of their playing children as a mother would be. A man is much more likely to allow his children to engage in "dangerous play," while an over-anxious mother lets her cautious desire for security and her desire to see her children safe turn her into a script-writer always imagining the worst-case-scenario. If the child climbs a tree, as children will do, her immediate response is "Come down from there – you're going to fall." She sees her child in hospital when he's up in that tree, and therefore she immediately tries to prevent that child from experiencing that climbing. There's research that suggests that if the child is not informed that they may fall, they are much less likely to fall. If they are warned that they might fall, they are statistically more likely to do so! It is a case of the over-anxious mother instilling insecurity in the child. And the fall will result in reinforcing the woman's sense of the danger that might befall the child in future. It will make her (and perhaps the child) even more cautious! A father, by contrast, is more likely to let the child take risks.

Regarding our development and design as men and women, the man's voice is very important for his role as protector. A man's deep voice carries (it has distance), whereas the sharp, high voice of a female doesn't carry (it's localised). In ancient times, the man's deep, booming voice was a big advantage to him as he occupied an overseeing position – in other words, guardianship – over those in his charge. He'd keep an eye out for danger, perhaps from a high point. The conversation that women had among themselves – in that localised voicing – wouldn't carry, and that was a very good thing because it served to protect them from outsiders listening who meant harm. If there was danger, the high-pitched scream was (and is) very effective at alerting a man. The booming sound of the male's voice, was (and is) very effective at warning off enemies.

Sadly, what you see happening in the world today is that there are men (albeit a minority), who, instead of standing at the door looking out and protecting their families and using their position to speak out, are instead standing with their backs to the door and speaking in and using their voices and strength to abuse rather than protect the household. It's very sad to reflect on this, because when this happens, a man is actually going against his very nature. You see little boys instinctively protecting their mothers when there is conflict between mum and dad. That can have long-term bad effects on the relationship between father and son, because it's a premature acting-out of his defensive role, but it is evidence of the protecting role that's in-born in men.

2) Is providing for his family a man's primary responsibility? Is it the thing that will make his wife and children feel most secure?

No. In our society over the past few hundred years, we've been led to believe that the man is the one who should be the primary breadwinner, the guy who puts the pay packet on the table, who farms the land and does the "work," but historically, from the very beginning, men and women shared the role of provision for the family. Traditionally, a man's role was for safety and security – building the fences, keeping away enemies and wild animals. The man wasn't the one that earned all the money. Yes, men did heavy labour and earned money, but it was equally the responsibility of the woman to bring in some resources. It was a combination of resources – both the woman's and the man's – that enabled the family to be fed and survive. If you think about it, in ancient times, the man was the hunter who went out with a pack of males to hunt down some beast to bring back meat, but the majority of the food would have been the grain and nuts and crops which were the domain of the gatherer woman. She sowed the seeds and remembered where the root vegetables and berries were as part of her collecting/gathering role. (Women have a greater ability to remember the location of items – you see it working in today's society when the mother is constantly asked by the husband and children: "Where are my socks? Where is my underwear?"!) The man was into the big macho killing of the beast which would only happen a few times a year compared to the regular food supplied by the woman. So he couldn't be thought of as the provider. Even the curing of the skin and the cutting up of the meat of the animal he brought back was the responsibility of the woman. The distribution of food generally was the domain of the woman. In this country on farms, that shared sense of labour would have been understood longer than in other western societies.

All this is a way of saying that the woman doesn't get her security from the finances a man provides. She gets it from his commitment to her and to his family. If the man is committed to that woman, she feels much more secure. It's when she feels that the commitment is not there and that the focus of care is not on her and her family that she feels insecure. Sadly, these days we don't see men committing to women as much as we would like. We see more predator males than committed males, and predator males are males that are terribly insecure and don't particularly want to make decisions. They often seek out strong females or females that will mammy them. They try to meet this desire to be mothered by giving themselves entirely into the care of the woman, just as little boys do in the early development stage. They have the expectation that this woman will do everything for them, including make decisions. These men are often described as an extra child in the family. And unfortunately, their behaviour is often controlling and bullying, because they want their woman all to themselves. By cutting her off from her friends and controlling her, the woman becomes isolated. The situation is made worse because these men often have an external presentation which is very pleasant, nice, kind and gentle. This type of male is often described as a misogynist, or a woman-hater, and these predator males are often boys that were never allowed to become men.

3) How important do you think good communication between the two parents is?

The husband and wife must discuss things related to the good of the children together. They should not be competing against each other for the children's affection. It's a sign of immaturity when a person is looking for affection or other needs to be met through the child. They want the child to accept them and not reject them, but your child is NOT going to reject you. They might temporarily say that they hate you or want nothing to do with you, but they actually want your favour all the time. So, when any decision needs to be made, it should be: "Your mother and I – or your dad and I – will have a chat about it and see where we need to go from here" – a united front. In fact, you really need to discuss a lot of this stuff even before you have children. When mothers and fathers come to me and say they have nothing to talk about when they go out to lunch alone together, I have to point out that there's no shortage of things to talk about. They should be discussing how they feel about the children and their own relationship and discuss all aspects around the children's development. To have a child is something that should be considered very carefully. It's dangerous to have children without thinking about it, because children are very demanding and very needy and to bring children into the world is an unselfish act. You're declaring that you'll put your life on the line that they might live. It's a very powerful experience, because it's not that you give up living but that you are prepared to sacrifice yourself that they might live.

Children are helped no end by seeing their mother and father getting along well together. They love to see their mother and father kissing or holding hands, for instance, even if they give out about it. It makes them feel very secure and it excites them. You're giving the children a very clear signal that things are alright. Children worry about their mothers and fathers naturally, and when they're at school with their peers, they hear and witness the results of family breakdown, all of which adds to those natural fears. It is therefore very important to send them positive signals, because the more reassurances they receive regarding the permanence of your relationship, the more secure they will feel.

Men and women need to communicate deeply with one another, but men are sometimes reluctant to open up. The main obstacle to men opening up is fear. They've lived most of their lives in the left hemisphere of the brain, and they are in the fixing/doing mode most of the time. The only time they usually switch over to the right side – the feeling side of the brain – is in the romantic times in their lives. And when they do so, it leaves them feeling very vulnerable. They feel threatened. It's not the place they want to go readily. One of the reasons sexuality is so powerful is that it forces men to engage with that emotional side of themselves. It is very important that men engage with their emotional side at times other than just sex, however, because it is there that they learn empathy and understanding and that they learn how to listen.

There are men whose levels of sensitivity are high and who don't mind opening up, due to the way they've been raised, and they're more scared by the practical side of things. These men who are emotionally charged are just as valuable as less emotionally-governed men, but just need some assistance with the practical, whereas the other men need help with the emotional. Traditionally, boys were expected not to show emotion because it showed a level of vulnerability in dangerous situations and was considered a weakness. I am glad that this is becoming a thing of the past, because today we see great, big rugby players being unafraid to show emotion, even on camera!

A statement that rings out to us from the past is "Wait till your father gets home!" In those days, the father had to come home and deal with justice. Children were filled with fear towards a very important character in their lives. The father was going to be told how bad you were, and he was expected to punish you in some way. And this caused huge problems in relationships between fathers and their children in the years to come. Dads were made out to be the baddies. Actually, statistically, it appears women commit more acts of violence towards children than men do. Sometimes mothers don't realise that the little slaps they give children spontaneously can have bad effects down the line, especially if they're done very often.

4) WHAT ARE THE FACTORS, IN YOUR EXPERIENCE, THAT LEAD MEN TO ABUSE THEIR WIVES AND/OR CHILDREN?

There are men who hit their wives but never touch their children or only hit their children and not their wives or only hit their sons and not their daughters. Emotional frustration caused by bottled-up emotion or unmet needs and a man's childhood experience of being hit at home or at school are often the causes of male violence towards their wives and/or children. Domestic violence is a big topic that could be covered alone as a book itself, but let me say here that men who find themselves in this position should really seek help, as the need to use any form of violence, either with your wife or your children, is deep-rooted in your own childhood, because hitting begets hitting. We know that children internalise traumatic events such as being hit and when a similar situation occurs as an adult with their own children, they can revert to this type of behaviour because they're seeing the event through the eyes of the child in them, not through the rational eyes of the adult. Breaking this cycle of violence requires professional help. You can be helped.

5) What is the biggest challenge facing a man as he prepares to start a family of his own?

As I pointed out earlier, the commitment that a man shows towards his partner and his children is extremely important in making his woman feel secure. That said, the biggest mental shift for a man upon getting married is the choice to truly commit. You can fall in love; you can be all kinds of sexy and all kinds of lustful, but commitment is a whole other thing. When you fall in love, you have all kinds of loving feelings flowing through you and that's very natural and normal because your testosterone level is going absolutely crazy through your system. We were created so that when we fall in love, there is an actual chemical reaction that causes us to be madly in love with somebody. But that isn't actually a preparation for marriage or fatherhood. Being a good spouse and then a good father requires a decision of the will to commit to that woman and your children no matter what may come.

Anybody can be a father but not many can become a daddy, because to be a daddy, you need to be committed to parenting and understand what your role is in your child's life. You need to value the contribution that you have to make to the new life that's been put in your care and understand how that new life will develop because of your input. So what I say to most men is that unless they really understand themselves and value who they are –

in other words, are really happy in their own skins – it's very hard for them to impart that kind of happiness to their children. The more and more you're content with yourself and with who you are, the more you're prepared for daddyhood as opposed to just fathering a child.

6) Does a man's childhood affect the way in which he will parent his own children?

How a man parents his own children is greatly affected by the model his own parents showed to him while he was growing up. Before the age of about ten, we interpret reality based on our feelings. "If I feel it, it must be true." Therefore, if our own father was distant, absent or violent, we are very likely to have decided that our father didn't like us and that all fathers are like that. A child doesn't naturally blame his parents. He decides that "My father must not love me because I am unlovable." If we believe we are unlovable and carry this lack of self-love into adulthood, it will certainly affect our ability to love our wives and children. So if you don't want to repeat the mistakes that were made with you, you must consciously decide to change your mind and heart, so that the bad relationship with your father or mother doesn't effect how you parent your own children. When each of us reaches 16 or 17, we become our own person, and after that it's important for all of us to have a look at our lives and value who we are and shed many of the labels that were put upon us when we were younger. We have to start looking at the positive aspects of ourselves. We all have positive and negative aspects but we can't just keep on beating ourselves up with negative attitudes toward ourselves. We need to understand that we are each unique human beings – a four hundred million to one chance (based on the number of sperm a man ejaculates) – and if we're a four hundred million to one chance then we really need to appreciate our uniqueness and not compare ourselves to other people because it's the comparisons that really damage us. Whether you're tall or short, whether you're sensitive or cautious, or whether you're an extrovert or an introvert, the thing you need to understand is that this is the cloth that you've been given and you must make the best suit you can out of it. Don't say that you wish you had been given some other piece of cloth, because that's never going to do you any good. To prepare yourself for the future, you really have to accept what you've been given, whatever that might be. And when you accept it and embrace it, stand in front of the mirror and look at yourself and say "Well, this is the only cloth I'm getting. And this is not a rehearsal; this is the real thing. And if I don't start caring and loving myself – by looking after my well being and seeing myself as a useful contributor to the world and to my family – then I will be a huge disadvantage to those that I have anything to do with because my negativity will influence them."

We grow up being constantly reminded to love our neighbour as we love ourselves, and when we hear that, we often fail to understand the "loving ourselves" aspect of the principle. We're more inclined to look at the needs and wants of others rather than ourselves. If we actually cared for ourselves the way we would care for a neighbour, we would treat ourselves with much more compassion. We'd be less hard on ourselves and much more forgiving. Thinking this way has many ramifications, so consider how you might love yourself better and realise that it's vitally important. Why is it important? Because out of the overflow of love we have for ourselves, we are able to love our neighbour. As you love yourself and genuinely care about yourself and value who you are, then that sense that you care that much for yourself overflows because it just emanates from you. And in that overflow, you communicate love for somebody else and have a stronger base from which to love someone else. This is especially true in marriage. If you love yourself well, then it means you won't be just giving yourself into your partner's care. Giving yourself into someone's care is not a good thing, because it's a huge burden for the other person to be responsible for <u>your</u> happiness. The ideal is for you to mutually <u>share</u> the love you have with your partner and they with you, creating an equal unity, less needy communication, and a very different kind of relationship. The only time that we are to give ourselves into the care of another person is in roughly the first 16 years of life, when we give ourselves into the care of our parents. It's a kind of unconditional delivery of ourselves – heart, soul, body – into their care as an acknowledgement that our parents are the ones who are responsible for our happiness and our well-being and our security at that time. It is the parents' responsibility to build us up into a person who can take over that responsibility for ourselves at a given time – 16-17 years of age.

a) Loving Ourselves Versus Low Self-Esteem

Many of us find it hard to love ourselves because we suffer from low self-esteem. Low self-esteem is usually the result of an individual not having their resources applauded. For example, if you happen to be a sensitive-cautious child and your parents look at that as being a huge disadvantage to you and they promote it as a disadvantage – saying "you shouldn't be shy," etc. – then what kind of message are you getting? You're getting the message that you're not what they want, and if you get that message into your head, you'll often try to be what you think they want and that leads you to behave in a way that's copying somebody else. And the more and more you become an actor rather than yourself, the more and more you'll see yourself as lying to yourself and to the world. You'll feel you're not being true to yourself and that the platform you're starting with is a lie. You'll begin questioning yourself, and your insecurity will start to be evident. Suddenly one day that whole persona that you designed for yourself will collapse. As a person, you either understand that you are the "I am" or you understand "I need to be somebody else." If you can accept that you are the "I am" then you have a much less difficult time than someone who is always striving to be somebody that they're not. In order to accept and love ourselves as we really are, we need to unclutter what we believe about ourselves by removing the lies which have been our truths since childhood. But before we are able to do that, we must first understand the intimacy needs of each child, because it was the denial of those intimacy needs in our own childhood that led us to believe those lies in the first place.

b) The Main Intimacy Needs

The main intimacy needs of each child work like a domino effect. The four primary intimacy needs have their secondaries, etc. But the primary ones have a foundational effect on how we live our lives. They are almost like the foundations of a house – our house, no matter how lovely, will fall unless it's built on rock. So it's a responsibility for a parent to make sure these healthy investments are made in their children. Your children will be demanding them at each stage of their development, and it's your job to recognise these needs and help to see that they're met.

The primary intimacy need is acceptance/forgiveness. We say forgiveness because we often feel accepted but only conditionally. We need to assure our children that they are loved unconditionally – "I will love you no matter what you do or what issues come up but please be open and honest with me. I love you and will forgive you." For children, there is a lesson to be learned from that acceptance/forgiveness process that enables them to accept and forgive others and themselves. The result of not having this need met is that they can be deceived into feeling that they are accepted but that it's conditional – i.e. "I'm accepted if I'm good and behave," etc. They end up being a people pleaser or someone who doesn't want to please people at all! So you can find children who are house angels and street devils or street angels and house devils. Their behaviour is more determined by the company they keep rather than by themselves. So to make children value who they are, they need to have acceptance that's unconditional. Otherwise, they live with the fear of rejection. "I'm not what my parents want, etc." When you believe that, it's a very painful and awful world to live in, because you're living at the behest of everyone else. You're inviting yourself to be a marionette while somebody else pulls the strings. How well a child feels accepted can be seen from how well you've gotten to know the child. When a child is loved unconditionally, they'll let you get closer. As a parent, remember that it's easy for children to believe that our love is conditional just because of the way we comment favourably or unfavourably on their behaviour. To a child, "You're a good boy" means "I'm loved" and "You've been a bad boy" means "I'm bad" because for them the world is very black and white. When a child is criticised for crying or displaying a need, they might decide "It's wrong to feel this way." They get all this "wrong" stuff in their heads so they strive to be "right" all the time and have an enormous fear of "wrong." And this can cause a child to be lacking in emotional response, because their fear of wrong paralyses them. They completely shut down because they have a childlike vision of wrong. They don't have a flexible understanding of right and wrong.

A good way of helping children feel accepted is to share something of your own past and childhood with them, including childhood pranks. This will cause them to feel the warmth of harmony with you, and that they're OK and not bad. Another important part of acceptance is to make them feel welcomed and greeted – that you're pleased to see them after an absence. Children also have a need to be believed as part of their need for acceptance, and they need to be able to bring their friends home and to share what they have with others. Acceptance brings a sense of permanency – that what they have at home is lasting – and this feeds a child's need for security.

The second main intimacy need is attention, and attention means listening. It means showing some care and affection and commenting favourably. And these things should be focused on your child personally – on their BEING, not their DOING. They should feel that what they have to say is important so that it gives them confidence to speak out in the future. This is important because it's so easy for them to interpret that what they have to say is not important. The fear of being ignored is a huge fear for children and it's a huge shame to wait till the brick comes through your window before realising "Hey, my child wants to be listened to."

The kind of actions that help the child internalise that they're receiving attention include showing caring concern by empathising with them in their hurts and showing kindness and compassion when they make their little mistakes. Being generous to them shows them that they have your attention, as does showering them with affection, which children respond very positively to. Be tactile, for closeness to your smell and the feeling of your touch, accompanied by the sound of your voice and loving facial gestures, all contribute to the message that you care.

HUGGING

Feels good

Dispels loneliness

Overcomes fear

Builds self-esteem (Wow! They actually want to hug me!)

Slows down ageing (Huggers stay younger longer)
Eases tension
Fights insomnia
Keeps arm and shoulder muscles in good condition
Is ecologically sound (Does not upset the environment)
Is democratic (Anyone is eligible for a hug!)
Is portable
Affirms physical well-being
Is energy efficient (Saves heat!)
Makes impossible days possible
Makes happier days happier

Author Unknown

The third intimacy need is encouragement. Encouragement is a strange one because we often think it means cheering people on and only doing that, but it also means comforting those who haven't succeeded. We have a big issue about that as parents, because we want the children to always be happy and hate to see them sad. When your little 8/9/10 year old plays a game and their side doesn't win, they're devastated by that. Saying, "Don't worry; you'll beat 'em next time" or "They cheated" or "Work harder next time" are all damaging phrases. What you need to do is put your arm around them and say, "I know how much you wanted to win and I know how important it was for you and I know how hard you worked to win but let me just give you a hug. It's going to be OK." Once you've identified with their feelings and their need to be comforted, they'll be much more likely to go out and try again next time. In any game, there's only one winner and the rest are losers, and that could be 15 guys on a team or even 30 guys on a track squad. They all participated to win, so if their objective was to win and they didn't and were disappointed by that, they need to be comforted so they don't feel like losers and have the courage to go again. Discuss future strategy later, particularly when the children are under ten years of age, because that's a time when they can easily interpret it as a criticism that they're not good enough and begin to believe that they're not good enough. Children aren't capable of thinking "This was just a game" but you are, because you're the adult. If they don't feel that comfort and encouragement, they may become fearful of criticism and become perfectionists or procrastinators or both. This may ultimately result in them not wanting to participate in anything.

Young children may appear dismissive about their failure to win at sport or succeed at some other activity. They're trying to test the water to find out how you react to certain events and to build up a library of information concerning how their parents handle disappointment. Though they may display a dismissive attitude, internally they are hurt because of the loss/failure and will need you to communicate that you're sad for them and understand how much they wanted to win/succeed. Give them that reassurance hug we discussed above. This type of response will give them the confidence to come to you to express their sadness and know it will not be purely dismissed. When their need for comfort isn't met, they can come to believe that it doesn't matter to you whether they win or lose and that their feelings aren't important, particularly their feelings of loss. They will conclude that they will only get attention when they succeed, because your response is always excitement at their successes.

In addition to comfort, encouragement also consists of coming alongside them and supporting their endeavour – be it a sport or some other activity. It consists of the teaching or training role you take in helping them overcome obstacles, because when you instruct and inspire them, it gives them hope that they have a future, that things aren't all gloom and doom. Promoting them in the presence of others is another very important part of encouragement. But always remember: to encourage effectively, you must withhold your personal fears from them, because they have enough fears of their own.

The fourth intimacy need is respect, and respect is a great word because it means "valued." The word has been used as a control device – children have easily interpreted "Respect your mother and father" as "Fear your mother and father" and that has done damage. But helping children understand that respect means "to value and see as precious" is the right way to go. They need to know that, to you and your partner, they are individually very special and a gift. That said, while it's very important for the child to see themselves as a gift, we must not make them little emperors. In China, that's a problem because of the one-child policy. Little boys feel like little emperors because they are so valuable and that's turned traditional Asian respect – based on age – on its head. We're not a million miles away from that here, so we must teach our children that respect is a two-way road. You respect the child and the child respects you. Teaching them that they're valuable makes them see that others are valuable, too. If you don't do it, they'll go around feeling or fearing worthlessness. When people are feeling worthless, they envy everyone else and would prefer to be someone else rather than themselves and that leaves them vulnerable to exploitation, etc. If they know that the person they are is valuable, it prepares them better for the future.

Your children will learn respect from seeing how you respect and value yourself, and how they see you respect others. Respect is one of those needs that helps you consider others and empathise with their situation, however difficult that might be. It helps you to admire and be admired, which in turn allows you to see yourself as worthy.

None of these four areas of investment is going to cost you money. Whether you live in a council house or a palace, when you invest these in your child, nothing should stop them from moving ahead in the world. They'll be a healthy individual with a healthy view of the world and other people. Because of this investment, you've shown them how to survive and thrive as they move into the future.

c) Assessing and Addressing Our Own Unmet Needs

If you are now feeling depressed because your childhood and the relationship you had with your mother or father left you with very little confidence in your own ability to parent, don't despair for help is at hand. We need to understand that in order to mature into adulthood, we must have our emotional, physical and spiritual needs met. And if we have not had these needs met appropriately, we will find ourselves with deficits in these areas. You may never have met your biological father or mother, because you were adopted or fostered or raised by one parent only. They may have been present but you never got to know them and fantasised about what it would have been like to be raised by some other family. The same fantasy methodology can be used in reengaging with yourself and parenting yourself using: 1) the leaving and cleaving; 2) the removal of the lies; and 3) the

FUNDAMENTAL NEED	HOW TO REINFORCE IT	IMPLICATIONS IF NOT MET
ACCEPTANCE / FORGIVENESS	1) Emphasise your love is not related to their behaviour	1) Having to please or do for fear of rejection 2) Becoming a slave to the needs of others and believing one has no choice 3) Diminution of self-worth
ATTENTION	1) Listening 2) Tactile Affection 3) Caring concern 4) Acknowledgement of them and what they're going through	1) Feeling "Nobody cares" 2) Feeling "What I have to say is not important" 3) Inappropriate understanding of touch
ENCOURAGEMENT	1) Assisting them 2) Comforting failures or losses 3) Promoting and applauding them 4) Speaking well of them in their hearing	1) Perfectionism 2) Procrastination 3) Low Self-esteem 4) A "Can't-Do" Attitude
RESPECT	1) Valuing them as unique and understanding their individual needs 2) Allowing them responsibility appropriate to their age	1) Worthlessness or Depression 2) Narcissism / Inflated belief in themselves / Self-obsession 3) Seeing others as more valuable or special than themselves

emotional inventory. But before we begin those processes, feel free to go to APPENDIX ONE (Childhood Questionnaire) to get a greater understanding of your own childhood.

i) Leaving and Cleaving

The child is designed, as we have already explained, to survive. And in order to do so the child will form special attachments. Science has shown that when a young boy is born, he has a stronger natural bond with his mother than with his father. Likewise, a mother will feel a stronger instinct to take care of her son than she will for her daughter. On the flip side, a daughter that comes into the world feels great natural affection towards her father, and her father feels a stronger natural bond with her. This is perfectly natural and there is nothing wrong with this. It is a normal part of each person's development. A son's strong bond with his mother continues for roughly the first eight years of his life. During this time, he has very protective feelings towards his mother, and his own nurturing, sensitive side is developed. At about eight years of age, he begins to emotionally distance himself from his mother and crosses over to his dad, and till he is around sixteen he learns from his dad "how to be a man." It's very important for Dad to be there for him at this time. On the other side, a girl's strong bond with her father in the early years of life includes her flirting with him and being "Daddy's girl." During this time, she learns how to interact safely with men and establishes her own sense of self in relation to his maleness. At about the age of eight, she begins to physically distance herself from her father because she's physically changing and becoming more aware of her own sexuality. It's written into her that she needs to move away from Dad at this time and cross over to her mother. The mother's role, until the girl is around sixteen, is investing the values of womanhood in her daughter and helping her develop her own sense of femininity.

If a boy doesn't bond with his mother early in life, he is at a huge disadvantage in future relationships with women as his need for attachment, which was firstly for his mum, may now be transferred to future relationships with women, where he may become controlling, obsessive and jealous of his partner.

If a girl doesn't bond with her father early in life, she may transfer that flirtatious energy towards other men, some of whom may be unsafe. If a father shuns the natural tactile intimacy that his little daughter craves, perhaps because it scares him, the girl will similarly not develop an appropriate relationship with men physically and may also end up in dangerous situations later on. Two notes about this: a father may sense himself being aroused when his little girl is cuddling up to him and it may scare him and cause him to shun physical contact with his little girl. He must understand that this arousal is a natural biological reaction to touch, no different than feeling aroused on a moving bus. As in the case of the bus, he must take charge over his body and say, "This is a natural biological response to touch/stimulation but it's not appropriate right now, so I must master it. It only means that everything is working." The second thing to note is that when a girl is bonding well with her father early in life, his wife may become jealous. It is very important for him to emphasise to his wife, his daughter and himself that though he loves his daughter dearly, his wife will always come first. One way to do this is to always greet your wife first when coming into the house, even though your daughter will run to you first when you get home.

At around the age of eight, a boy may not cross over to his dad for several reasons. His father may not be around, due to work or because he no longer lives with the family. It may be because his father is a very angry person and therefore the son is too scared to approach the father. It may be that the boy is sensitive and artistic and that the father would prefer if his son were more macho and into sport, etc., and therefore he doesn't really know how to relate to his son. Or it may be that the father is jealous of the bond between the boy and his mother. A boy sometimes doesn't cross over because the mother is holding on to him too tightly. In this case, she is getting her emotional needs met through her son, because her husband is not there for her emotionally, and so she doesn't want to "lose" her son, who has become an emotional crutch. Whatever the reason, not crossing over has many effects on a boy's development. He may not develop his own sense of manhood and self. He will have an undelivered "package of love" to give to another man, and if he doesn't give it to his father, he will often give it – sometimes emotionally, sometimes physically – to another man. Also, because a boy naturally pulls away from his mother in his teen years, if he is still tied too strongly to his mother, he may begin to treat her with disrespect as a natural defence mechanism, and it may be the birth of lifelong misogyny.

If a girl doesn't cross over to her mother at about eight, she may remain as "Daddy's little girl," which may leave her emotionally immature, wanting her partner to be more of a minder/ Daddy to her than a husband. She may confuse the husband/

Daddy roles, constantly comparing all males with her father. This type of female may go on to have children, but her demand for attention will exceed that of her children and give the wrong signals to the children that their needs are meant to be ignored. She also, like the man who doesn't cross over, may end up with an undelivered "package of love" for a woman, which can later result in her developing an emotional/physical relationship with another woman.

At around sixteen years of age, young men and women want to take this accumulated security and knowledge that's been invested in them and go into the world with the ability to share their abilities and qualities with a meaningful other. If the process of giving yourself into the care of your mother and father and finally leaving your mother and father is not fulfilled, the young adult will be still trying to have his or her needs met by giving themselves into the care of another later in life. They will expect their partners to meet their every need, which can lead to childlike behaviour in adults. As such, it is important that all of us successfully go through the process of leaving our mothers and fathers, so that we can join together with a meaningful other, secure in who we are, not depending on the other for our happiness. As the mind is a wonderful place and our creativity and power of fantasy are important parts of our neurological development, we can use a cognitive method of renewing our minds by completing the following exercise:

We are all born as gifts to our parents and we have in us a desire to love these parents unconditionally, but we need the opportunity to deliver this love and it seems there is an orderly way this is done. When a young boy looks at his mother, he will often feel, "I want to marry my mammy when I grow up." Even if you weren't raised with your biological mother, this desire to love your mother remains until it is fulfilled. And the young girl feels the same about her dad. She may say, "I want to marry my daddy when I grow up." This changes as a child reaches around eight years of age, when children automatically want to distance themselves from the opposite sex parent and cross over to the same sex parent. To commence the cognitive process of giving that unconditional love to the parents, consider you are a young child coming up to your eighth year. Imagine yourself saying to your mother that you love her very much. Say these words to her: "Mum, I love you very much and I want to give myself into your care so that you might teach me to be the man and son that I am designed to be, but I have been really hurt by not having some of these emotional needs met." In the case of the young boy who's had these needs met but been overly mothered in a smothering way, you may have been left feeling very helpless and left feeling that women are very demanding. In your case, say, "Mum, I love you very much and I want to give myself into your care so that you might teach me to be the man and son that I am designed to be but I have been really hurt by the over-indulgence you've shown me." For the person who's never know their biological mother, say, "Mum, I love you very much and I want to give myself into your care so that you might teach me to be the man and son that I am designed to be, but, as I have not been able to do this, I have been very hurt." Then you should say, "Because I love you, I forgive you, but I must say goodbye to you now." Imagine that you are letting go of her hand and bringing the next unconditional love package to your dad. Declare to him that, "Dad, I love you very much and I want to give myself into your care so that you might teach me to be the son and the man I am designed to be." If your dad did not accept that love from you and therefore did not invest the teaching in you, you need to say, "I have been very hurt by not having received this affirmation of who I am from you, but because I love you, I forgive you and I must say goodbye." This brings you to the final love package, which is for yourself, where you see yourself as a sixteen year old and declare love for yourself and forgive yourself for not loving yourself. Promise to love yourself unconditionally. This gives you the opportunity of parenting yourself, appreciating the little child in you that may not have been understood, the teenager in you that rebelled, and the young man who was left confused regarding his true self. All of those younger versions of yourself will now be unconditionally embraced by you as you exercise that unconditional love in your day to day living, a love that appreciates you as a human being rather than a human doer, a human doer being someone who tries to please people to be accepted and loved.

ii) Removing the Lies

During the first ten years of our lives, our interpretation of what's happening all around us is governed by emotional reasoning – that is, "If I feel it, it must be true" – which leads to internal beliefs about ourselves and others which are often founded on feelings rather than facts. For example, "I feel that my teacher doesn't like me." That might not seem so bad, but when you feel that you're not what others want you to be, it can cause you to conform to what everybody else wants in order to be accepted. Thinking that you're a bad boy or worthless or stupid are the kinds of thoughts that are often put into our foundational beliefs about ourselves, never to be questioned again. And, later on in life, we find ourselves unable to receive compliments or encouragement because the words being said to us don't match the words we have already imbedded in our thought processes. The need to revisit and re-examine those foundational beliefs is an important part of our maturity. It leads to our ability to love ourselves and one another better. Feel free at this point to go to APPENDIX TWO (Removing The Lies), in order to engage in this re-examination and removal process.

iii) Emotional Inventory

Now that you have a greater understanding of your childhood and the main intimacy needs, you are in a much better position to assess how the denial or fulfilment of those needs in childhood still affects your relationships today. To assist you in this, you can now go to APPENDIX THREE (Emotional Inventory).

It is important to understand that often in childhood, when the emotional needs are unmet, just like the "sour grape syndrome", we may decide to reject that particular need, which can be for us a blind spot in our relationships with others. For example, as our need for support went unmet, we are often inclined not to seek support and therefore be critical of others needing support. On the other hand, there may be another need that you are always trying to fulfil in all of your relationships. If you have an "I-have-to" mentality with regard to that need, you will be inclined towards acting out roles in order to have that need met. For example, a person with an "I-have-to" mentality might complain about all the things they have to do just so that people give them attention. If you have an "I-choose-to" mentality, you will have the freedom to receive that need when appropriate but at the same time not feel that it has to be met at all costs.

Helen, a female client of mine, felt that her marriage was full of "Have-to's." She felt that she had no choice when it came to all the tasks around the house, because, if she didn't do them, the house would fall apart. She therefore got no satisfaction or joy from doing those tasks for her family or from being a housewife. She was close to separating from her husband, feeling he wasn't helpful (he would just come home from work and watch the telly) and that the children were not cooperative either (they wouldn't put things away when asked, etc.). All this became too much for her and she decided she wanted out. That's when she came to me. When we began to discuss her childhood, she explained that, as a young girl, she didn't have choice when it came to household tasks. She was loaded with responsibility, because she was the second girl in a large family and saw herself as "Mammy's little helper." She felt that she had no choice about playing that role in her childhood home and, when she married, she instinctively continued playing the same role. When I talked to her about things she enjoyed doing and asked her whether she had to do them or chose to do them, she recognised the difference between having-to and choosing-to. I explained that she needed to separate herself from the doing of these tasks. When she did that, she would be able to make choices about what she wanted to do. She would be able to see that things needed to be done and that she was making the choice to do them or not do them. The feeling of what she had to do became less of a burden. The mind is opposed to the instruction of having-to because we associate it with all the unpleasant things we were forced to do growing up. But when we consider these tasks as things we've chosen to do, we find our minds put up much less resistance.

As I've said before, all of the intimacy needs are normal and healthy. It's important to understand that your children and spouse will want to have these needs met, even though they might not always be aware of their need. To assist you in understanding each other's needs, it's a good idea to fill out the Emotional Inventory Questionnaire in APPENDIX THREE with other family members, if you haven't done so already.

7) How have you found that abuse of alcohol affects a family?

It takes four or five generations to get alcohol addiction out of a family. And our Irish ancestors, being a downtrodden people with not much going for them, found alcohol to be a very attractive escape. Years ago, they didn't have Prozac and other medications to deal with the depression, so our ancestors relied on "the old reliable" – alcohol. They knew that if they took a few glasses of beer or whiskey, they'd enter an altered state that would take away the pain of their miserable existence – an existence in which even the next day's meals were in doubt. They created a society that celebrated the drink, and celebrated the Paddy who, despite being very depressed in every day life, could become the life and soul of the party after a few drinks. This applauding of alcohol occurred because alcohol lifted the spirits of those who were suffering, but we are not a downtrodden society anymore, so we must stop our ongoing desire to self-medicate.

We criticise our ancestor's drunkenness but the survival of many of the men depended in their being able to get out of their heads. The alcohol helped them to bear another week or another year of misery and hardship. It helped them to deal with the deaths of some of their children or to deal with the fact that their eldest child took the boat and that they'd never see him or her again. There was a melancholy that needed a cure, and alcohol provided it.

The way teenagers get drunk today is no different from what would have been done in the past. Years ago, the men would have gathered together at a fair after selling a bullock or cow and get themselves absolutely blotto – hence, the caricatures in Punch Magazine and other publications depicting the drunken Irish. All you'd see on a Saturday evening were these fellas falling around the place, legless. They'd go home to a wife who had to make herself available to them, and then they'd soon find that there was another child on the way. In the end, good things came of a not-so-great situation. The very large families helped economically, because it often required many to work together to make a success of the household. Also, because of disease and sickness, many of the children would die, so there was a survival/self-preservation aspect to it as well.

It is my opinion that young people today drink too much because they don't know where they're going. Their life feels almost pointless. The young women don't know if they're ever going to meet somebody who's willing to commit themselves to a relationship, and yet they're frightened by what they've seen in the relationship between their parents. Divorce is a reality here now, so there's no security in relationships anymore. Men and even women are not prepared to commit to one another and yet there's an instinct in us that wants to commit so that we can engage in procreation and bring new life into the world. So there's a struggle within and between men and women. And how do they deal with the despair connected to that struggle? Many young men and women go to the pub and drink to excess, because for a very short time, they might have absolutely no memory and block out the unpleasant things in life.

Men may also be getting drunk because a man naturally sees himself as a doer and a fixer, so he feels he must do, fix, and sort things out. That's what makes him feel such a keen sense of responsibility for the welfare of his family. When a man abdicates his responsibility (either due to losing his job or some other factor), then he can become very lost. And how does he deal with the despair of losing his ability to do, to fix, to sort things out? He'll often end up crying into his pint, lost in a sense of helplessness.

8) Are men adversely affected by pornography?

Porn has been around for a long, long time, and because men are designed to be aroused by what they see, porn plays a huge role in some men's lives. Looking down through the centuries, there was a time when just seeing a woman's ankle would send a man into all kinds of ecstasy. And at the time when ankles were such a turn-on, breasts would be hanging out all over the place. Men, by nature, find what is NOT seen to be the turn-on, so we've always played with the idea that what is covered up is more titillating than what's exposed. On the other hand, there are people who walk around beaches naked and it doesn't cause them any disturbance because they've learned to use their minds correctly. Instead of the myth that our brain is between our legs, these people are using their heads and controlling their impulses. Because of the way we're designed, we can become aroused just walking down the street or travelling on the bus, but we know that when we get turned on walking down the street, we mustn't try to have sex with the lamppost. We learn how to manage that arousal. We must develop the appropriate management of our arousal and sexuality. In the meantime, people will look at sexy magazines or movies out of sexual curiosity or use sexual arousal as a comforter. The part of the brain that's stimulated by sexual arousal is the same part that's stimulated by alcohol or cocaine or heroin, so there's not a great deal of difference between them. They're all addictions that make you want to keep repeating the same sensation in your brain.

The use of porn as a stimulant for your sexuality demands that you start down the road of disrespecting the object of your arousal and that may affect the way in which you see your partner. Also, porn is an abusive application of the naked body, so people who view porn now have been seeking out images that are more and more explicit and de-humanising. They become tired of one extreme and so they go on to the next one and so on. It's just like when you take the first snort of cocaine and get out of your head.

The next time you decide to do a line and a half in hopes of generating the same high. People who view porn will likewise always demand more and more and more. Like any addiction, the person needs support and professional help for a successful recovery.

SECTION TWO

parenting small children

1) What does a man need to know about his newborn baby?

There is a plethora of publications describing the infant's developments from Day 1 onwards, detailing when you might expect to see their first tooth and when they will be expected to walk and to talk, etc. Such books, written by eminent and highly-qualified doctors and psychologists, are widely available and should you need that type of information, there are many books that could do the job. My endeavour here, however, is to inform you about the emotional needs of the child, which aren't always visible to the eye. You notice when your child isn't eating or walking or talking, but it's much more difficult to see their emotional needs. The children themselves will give you very broad hints, but if you don't know what to look for, you could very well miss them, especially if you are a parent who did not have your own emotional needs met in childhood.

With regards to babies, one area I do want to cover is a baby's sense of attachment to its parents. The signature scent of our birth mother is indelibly marked in our brains. The part of our brain that deals with emotion is near the nose, so when we smell that signature scent it goes straight to that place and makes us feel safe. If you have any prolonged distancing from that scent, it can – depending on the particular child – have traumatic effects. It was French researchers who first discovered that the mother has a signature scent and that a scent connection exists between the mother and child. They found that if you put day-old infants in the middle of a circle of women, they'll wriggle their way towards their natural mother, no matter where she is in the circle. The child that doesn't move at all is the one whose mother is not present. That kind of evidence says that the child does know its mother and has identified with her. In the same way, research has found that when a child presents itself at the mother's birth channel, it stimulates a part of the mother's brain that creates an attachment with the baby. As a result, mothers can have all kinds of difficulties when they want to leave that baby with someone else. Before having the baby they may have said, "I'll leave it with my mother or my sister," but then find they can't do it. These new mothers find it very distressing to have to leave the baby and go to work. It's a sense of attachment they've never experienced before. Likewise, many women say "I'll never have big conversations about my baby" because they were bored out of their trees when meeting friends who had recently become mothers, but when they have their own child they find that the baby is all they want to talk about. "The baby's doing this and the baby's doing that and the baby's smiling and it's so exciting!" These women find they have a whole new way of looking at children and thinking about children because of the way they're designed.

Just as women find it hard to leave their new babies, the babies react badly to any break in the scent connection with its mother.

There is research from Holland to suggest that children shouldn't be separated from that scent for more than twenty hours. A wonderful (and true) old wives tales is for the mother to work up a good sweat and leave some garment under the pillow so that you can spend longer away from the child without it stressing the child. One of my clients had a new baby and I had already told her about the signature scent, so when she had to be rushed back to the hospital, she gave plenty of her underwear and clothes to the husband for the baby. And the baby was very much at ease for the week she was away! It kept the child in contact with the scent. The closest thing to the mother's scent is the scent of the mother's mother, so if you're fortunate enough to have the child's maternal grandmother around and you have a good relationship with her, that's a very good place to leave the child and for the child to find comfort. If a father is present at the birth of his child, a strong scent connection is made with him as well. This scent factor is crucial up to about three years of age. After that, children get a bit more independent and less anxious about being close to their mothers and fathers.

(Just as a side note, another example of how scent is so important to children can be seen in the fact that many children hold on to a "comforter" that has a familiar smell that they can put up to their nose and feel safe. They don't want it washed. They just want that smell that says, "I feel safe.")

We're all born very different and with different levels of sensitivity. How we react to any given situation depends on our sensitivity. As such, different results occur when a baby is separated from its mother's signature scent for a prolonged period, depending on the sensitivity of the particular child. I have called the trauma that some babies experience when separated from the birth scent Infantile Post-Traumatic Stress Disorder (iPTSD). Bolby, Ainsworth and many other researchers in attachment theory did great work on separation anxiety but didn't go all the way back to the trauma caused by separation from that signature scent. As I've explained, a mother's signature scent is like a fingerprint and it's unique to that woman and it's emblazoned on the brain of her infant, and it's what that child identifies with its safety and security. Although the child is out of the womb, it's attached to the "invisible umbilical" of that birth mother for the first three years of life. If the child is separated from that scent, trauma can occur, and can cause the child to live defensively and see the world as hostile. A lot of antisocial activities – like acting out and aggression – can be the result of this type of trauma. As children under three who experience trauma will not have an expressible memory of the event (their memory or library of events is only being developed), the child has only feelings to rely on, and the feeling they most often experience and express is that something terrible is going to happen. The traumatised child begins to interpret that something could happen to mum and dad or that they themselves may die. This feeling that something bad is going to happen can start the process of being hyper-sensitive, startled at sudden noises. Their imagination begins to see the world as more hostile and they start developing a mistrust of strangers and strange situations. This child is likely to display a very defensive attitude towards most things and find it difficult to accept closeness. They become more and more independent, trying to work things out for themselves. Later, they're reluctant to speak about unhappy events such as death, dying or separation, and when such things are discussed, it can make them have bad feelings towards mums, dads and siblings, leading to outbursts of anger followed by bouts of remorse. They end up with a feeling of not belonging – strangers in their own home. The child will need therapy in healing this condition. The child needs to have someone explain that they're in that defensive mode and that they have authority over it and can switch out of it. And with professional help that's possible. Some children are diagnosed with ADD and ADHD when in fact it's more likely to be "infantile post-traumatic stress disorder" (iPTSD).

2) What should parents watch out for as their young children prepare to start school?

In Ireland, unlike other parts of Europe, it is quite common for boys and girls to start school at the age of four. By that age, an Irish child may have had playschool or Montessori or something similar – all of which have levels of benefit for the child – but studies have shown that he or she is not developmentally ready to begin the type of learning that most schools require. And what's more, boys and girls develop and learn differently, so they will each struggle in different ways.

Let's take the boy as an example. There are two hemispheres of the brain, and for young boys, communication between the two hemispheres is very narrow. This causes young boys to focus on the left side of their brain, and means that the way they see the world is very linear. Because most boys process information in a linear way, they find lateral processing much more difficult, and lateral processing is what is involved in reading, writing and spelling. As a result, many young boys struggle with reading, writing, and spelling, and resist doing work on them at this early stage, because they find such work so difficult. Their resistance can cause trouble for them with teachers and parents, all of which can make school a source of trouble for the child in the home. Moving into the future, such a boy may carry a belief with him that he is no good at reading, writing and spelling, and that belief – based on a child's conviction that "If I feel it, it must be true" – will negatively affect his life long into adulthood. If that boy were to start reading and writing later – at say seven or eight, when lateral processing becomes a bit easier for boys – he'd be in a much better position to start learning those skills.

Young girls, in contrast to boys, have difficulty with the linear processing because they are much more lateral in their thinking. They are what scientists call "bridge-brained" – in other words, the left and right hemispheres of their brains communicate very well with each other due to the fact that their connection is wider. As a result of this, reading, writing and spelling are much easier for a young girl than for a young boy. Her difficulty with linear thinking, however, means that she may find addition, subtraction and other maths very difficult, and will often beat herself up emotionally over it. She'll interpret – again with a child's emotional reasoning – that she's no good at maths, and that's why we see so many adult women today who really believe that they're no good at maths. I believe we have lost a whole nation of woman who could do very well at the sciences just because early on they decide that they are no good at mathematics. (When taken into account with the men whose hand-writing skills might become a barrier to producing the kind of essays required to pass exams – due to the fact that examiners cannot read their work – we see why there is such an imbalance in certain fields between the sexes.) These women would be much better off if they were started on mathematics at age seven or so, when linear processing becomes a bit easier for them.

There are other conditions that may cause the boys or girls to have learning difficulties, including infantile Post-Traumatic Stress Disorder (iPTSD), which we discussed earlier.

Because boys and girls learn so differently and have different struggles, research has shown it is of greater benefit for them to go to single-sex schools, where their different approaches to learning can be catered for and where there is no temptation to compare boys with girls. It's not a good idea to compare, for instance, your four-year-old son with your daughter when she becomes four. They'll have different ways of approaching tasks and different natural obstacles to learning. This might have been the case with you. If you found that you did not write or spell or add or subtract as well as your brother or sister, you might have gone on to dislike these subjects – that is, unless or until you had a teacher whom you liked and who helped you to overcome those fears.

3) IN YOUR EXPERIENCE, WHAT'S THE BEST WAY FOR PARENTS TO ASSIST THEIR CHILDREN WHEN THEY GET STUCK WHILE LEARNING A PARTICULAR LESSON OR TASK?

As all children – male or female – grow and learn, they will occasionally reach certain points where they get stuck and can't go on without the input of a teacher or a parent. Vygotsky, in his theory of the "Zone of Proximinal Development," has argued persuasively that what these children need is a "leg up" to get to the next stage, and once they do, they'll be away again, moving on to greater heights. Parents need to understand this. If they watch out for times when their child gets stuck and give them that little bit of help – without condemnation – it triggers a whole bunch of information that enables the child to go on. I'm sure you can understand this, as it happens to us all. We cannot live in isolation; we need each other so that when we get stuck, someone will be there to provide the leg-up and help us soar away again.

4) HOW IMPORTANT, DO YOU THINK, IS THE ROLE A FATHER PLAYS IN ENCOURAGING HIS CHILDREN AS THEY GROW AND LEARN?

The father plays a crucial role in giving the children a sense of secure identity. They need that father stamp of approval. It's so important for a father to acknowledge the child and to make statements of encouragement to the child. Because the nurturing mother will often comment favourably about her son or daughter, the child can assume "Well, mum is always going to say nice things anyway" and take it for granted. By contrast, children hang on the few words of encouragement from the dads. The woman's bridge-brain, being more developed in the areas related to the voice and voice development, find speaking easier. As a result, they have the capacity to speak 26,000 words per day, which men often complain about! The man, on the other hand, can only manage 16,000. And some men don't use any of their allotment, about which women often complain!

It seems that something in human nature means we respond to confirmation. If somebody says "You look well," you may just take that as being a polite gesture, but if you visit a supermarket that same afternoon and the supermarket attendant says "You know, you're really looking well," you're more inclined to believe it. When it's coming from two different sources, you believe it, whereas if it's only coming from one, the words just sort of disappear. So the mother AND the father have to comment favourably on the child.

5) How do children regard promises from their parents?

Promises from a parent are sacred to a child. An example of that in my own life is when I asked my 34-year old son Kevin, "Was there anything I ever did that caused you to be very disappointed?" And he said, "Yes, you promised to make me a go-cart and you didn't." I remembered the occasion he was referring to. I had been given this ride-on mower and I was going to strip it down and make a go-cart out of it, but subsequently, I repaired it and gave it to my dad because he had a lot of grass to cut. I hadn't realised that Kevin was really gutted because he had probably seen himself in his dreams tearing around the garden in this go-cart his dad was building for him. As parents, we don't realise that children perceive promises from a mother or father as things that are definitely going to happen. They don't understand that it may have been a throwaway remark or that you might say one thing just to get out of something else. Children hold you to what you've said. They'll scream, "You said you would! You said you'd bring me there!" And this leads to all kinds of problems when you have couples that are divorcing or separating. The children are already feeling insecure about their world – especially if they're under ten – so when a parent says "I'll be there at six" but then doesn't show, the child is very heartbroken. As far as the child is concerned, the promise you will pick them up is THE LAW; it's a FACT. It's not "I might be there to pick you up" or "I might be there at six," and they can be very, very hurt at this time. Likewise, I hadn't realised that my own son was really hurt by my not making him the go-cart I promised; he felt that this was the worst thing that had happened to him in his life. I'm sure there were things that were an awful lot worse – or more damaging – but for him personally, that incident felt like the worst thing that had ever happened to him. I promised him something and hadn't delivered, and now he had to ask himself "Who can I believe anymore? Whose promises can I rely on?"

6) Is it important that we love each child the same way?

I believe that every child is uniquely different, and therefore each have to be met where they are and in accordance with their own unique needs/personality. Saying "I love all the children the same," is an unhelpful statement to make and a lie. By loving each child differently in a way that suits them specifically, you are giving them an identity and valuing them for who they are. Always remember that you are the one in the best position to know your child well, and you MUST take the time to get to know them. I can't emphasise that enough. You should be looking at their talents, their abilities, their qualities, their personalities. This will help you parent them in the way that's best suited to their needs.

Not only is every child of yours unique, they each have a different mother and father, because a child's reaction to the same parent will always be different than its sibling's. And each child will try to find its own space within the family. Our primitive instincts will mean that our position in the family will determine how we react to the other members of our family, and the roles we instinctively take on are not always good for us or for the others. Parents must intervene and make sure we don't fall into roles that could cause damage within relationships. Investment from parents, assuring the children that they are all unique and special, will avert many of the problems associated with position in family. We must keep our children from attacking one another by explaining that all children instinctually behave in a defensive, primitive way towards one another because of ancient survival mechanisms. These mechanisms date back to a time when siblings might have had to kill each other in the competition for limited food resources! (Reassure your children that you are available to each of them, that the fridge is full, and that there is enough food for all!)

Ordinarily in families, the first boy will gravitate towards mum if that's allowed and it's important for him to do so. And if the first child is a girl, she'll gravitate towards dad. Problems can arise when child number two comes along. If child number two is the same sex as its older sibling, it's a competing situation. If it's a boy, the second boy may not have the same access to the mother, especially if they're close in age. He'll see himself as excluded from the family circle on some level. If it's a second girl, the first girl will usually be dominant, so the second girl will gravitate towards the mother and becomes "mammy's little helper" – pleasing and helping mammy. When the third child comes along, he or she will often attempt to be a peacemaker between the first two siblings. Families build themselves in groups of three – first, middle and last child followed by first, middle and last child and so on. The first and fourth children will behave similarly and often get along well, the second and fifth children will be independent/observers (which can be good or bad) and the third and sixth will be the peacemakers. Of course, there are exceptions to these patterns based on the character of the individuals involved. For example, if the first girl is especially sensitive and shy, she may be the "mammy's helper" because she's more cautious in her approach to daddy, especially if he's "scary" – raises his voice, etc. – in any way. And the second, more outgoing girl in that case would gravitate towards dad.

As a family therapist, it has been my observation that where you're placed in the family may have implications as to what intimacy needs are met or unmet. For example, if you are the eldest, your need for affection might be omitted but you're given responsibility which means that your need for respect will be well met. As a result, you may specifically seek out affection in your relationships in the future and become upset if your need for affection is dismissed. If you happen to be the second child in a three child family, depending on the spacing of the children and the gender, you might find yourself feeling that you are not being given enough attention. Therefore, because you feel ignored, you may decide that you are not what your parents want. This can lead to the child becoming independent and self-reliant. The third child in a three children family will often be the child who expresses the most neediness, leading to them being treated as "the baby." Another common pattern is that it appears that first children often get all the responsibility and none of the freedom, third children get all the freedom and none of the responsibility and second children feel like they have to do it all by themselves.

Huge difficulties can arise from these natural roles that children take on so it's very important for parents to intervene and smooth things over between siblings. If we intervene, then, in the long run, the whole family will get along in a much happier, more peaceful way.

My own experience was one that was an exception to the rule. I'm the eldest of ten children and the first boy. Whereas I felt like a typical first child in that I had all the responsibility, I also felt while growing up that my mother favoured my younger brother over me, as he was deemed to be very good-looking. A favourite dinner time story when we had guests was that I was the first and they improved on the rest. And when my mum and dad spoke of their first reaction to my coming into the world, they said "We're no oil paintings, but what an ugly baby!" This comment reinforced my belief that I was not what they wanted and subsequently at the age of fourteen, I went to live with an aunt rather than stay within my own family group when they moved to France. I have no doubt now that my parents never meant to harm me or to cause me any form of distress, because later on in my life, having shared this concern with my mum, she was horrified to think that I saw myself as not important in her eyes and assured me that I was very much loved by her and my dad. The consequence of my internal belief was that I didn't really get to know my parents until I was in my forties and my mum and Dad moved back from France to Ireland. My position in the family and my feelings about myself and the family were governed by my interpretation of what was being said at those dinner parties and on such occasions. My view that my brother was the favoured one remained until he and I became friends on his 50th birthday! And so my own personal experience was quite contrary to that of typical first child, who is often seen as the favoured one. Later, as I studied the subject of childhood and child development, I came across a study of children who are stressed during childbirth and in the study their little faces were often described as crunched-up and old-looking and not placid and serene. My mother's experience of my birth was traumatic and I was the only child of hers to be born in a hospital. Her experience at the hospital was so unsatisfactory that she decided to have home births for the remaining nine children.

We need to be very careful about comments we make in the children's presence that are negative, as a children's childhood is governed more by their interpretation of reality, an interpretation which can be erroneous and therefore negatively affect how they see their parents, their siblings and the world.

7) Is there an appropriate way to prepare existing children for the arrival of a new baby?

There's nothing more wonderful than the birth of a new child! However, parents should be aware that while the new arrival needs to be greeted with excitement and joy, the child that's already present may feel threatened. To help to remove this threat, it is a good idea to give a present on behalf of the newborn to the older sibling. This often unites them as friends and removes the older child's fear of being ignored, which is often overlooked by parents because of the excitement they're experiencing over the new baby.

8) Is there a different way of addressing the needs of twins or multiple births?

In the past it was common to have twins dress identically, and when discussing this practice with the twins later on in life, they have confirmed that such a practice made them feel as though they were the same and not unique. My recommendation, based on what my twin clients have said, is that they should be dressed differently and considered to be different, remembering that internally they ARE different. In brain scans, the layout of the right and left hemisphere of their brains is different, so, although they might be physically alike and might have similar desires and wants, their individuality needs to be respected and cherished in the early development stages.

9) Have you suggestions as to how I can teach my children to be responsible while at the same time giving them more freedom than I had growing up?

In the 1950's and 60's and before that, many children were brought up with huge responsibilities but no freedom. Unfortunately, we are now suffering the backlash of that. We are seeing an enormous number of children who are brought up with all the freedom and very little responsibility. And this new phenomenon is responsible for many of the ills we see today. Children are much more secure when given responsibility and defined limits. We need to understand that children as young as six and seven in other societies take on great responsibilities. We don't want child labour or to have our children take on too much, but many of us feel we should keep our children from roles of responsibility until they are 15 or 16 or 17 and by then it's too late. They won't entertain the thought of taking on responsibility then!

The responsibilities you place on each child should depend on what you perceive to be an appropriate role for your child in the house, taking their age and personality and circumstances into account. For example, if a child is two and is just starting to walk and has been playing with the pots under the sink, you should help them to understand that putting the pots back is a responsibility. Introduce the responsibility of putting them back as a game, and show them how pleased you are with their help. If you are showing a small child how to pick things up and put them in the bin, don't worry if they put good things in the bin. As with the example of the pots, treat the responsibility of putting things in the bin as a game. It teaches them a responsibility and shows them how a house functions properly. It also teaches them that the house should be a safe environment for you and for them. Keep on reminding yourself that you didn't learn a sense of household responsibility by accident – it was taught to you somewhere in your own development stage. (If it wasn't, then you really need to learn it now!) So as early as possible, as soon as the children start to move around the floor – on their bottoms or hands and knees or whatever – engage them in the "play" of doing chores. Bring them to the kitchen sink when you're washing up and let them dry dishes. If your child is helping you wash the dishes or clear the floor or preparing food, you need to give them time and understand that they're only at the learning stage. A lot of them feel very awkward and nervous about things that they are asked to do, and they can easily develop a can't-do attitude. If your child is developing a can't-do attitude, it's because you've hurried them into a task. Nobody learns hurriedly. If they are forced to work quickly, they become very confused about the task, and if they are criticised over how they've done a new task, they will become very discouraged. You must have patience with the child. When teaching them a task, it will take much longer than if you had done it yourself, and that's because the child is taking that long to learn and it needs to be allowed to take longer. Many parents will say to their child who is assisting them with the washing-up "I'd have it done 10 times faster myself! Will you just step down!" or, if they've asked them to do a task, they'll often come back in and say, "Have you not done it yet?!?" and "Why hasn't it been finished?!?" These parents will go on and on and on and nag and nag and nag about the way in which the job was done. Meanwhile, if they were working for an employer that didn't train them properly or give them the time to learn, they'd be very upset. They'd report it to the union and wouldn't really fancy going into that job. Your children are intelligent and they're bright and they're learning all the time, and the person that is the best teacher in the house is you. If you want your children to learn well then you've got to give them the time, and giving them time means you've got to understand their strengths and weaknesses and take them into account as you train them. They'll follow your lead and instructions, but if you are assuming that they'll have this miraculous ability to be wonderful at washing dishes and tremendous at hoovering the floor and to be as good as you at any of the tasks around the house then you are missing the whole point. You'll get them so upset that they'll want to give up and not do the job. You are going to make them fear criticism as they start new tasks. They won't feel a sense of encouragement from you, and, as I've said, encouragement is one of the basic intimacy needs of all children. The fear of criticism and sense of discouragement will lead a sensitive child to do twice as much work in any of their efforts at school, because they're frightened of not getting their exercise correct or they're frightened of criticism from the teacher and from others. This is made worse if they are made to feel ashamed at home or singled out at school for not having something done correctly. So, as you can see, parents are essential teachers in a child's life. They are teaching their child the best way to live in the world for themselves. They are teaching them how to be more secure and to develop a can-do attitude. Your child should be going into the world with the attitude that "I can do it but I need to have the training for the doing of it. I know that if I get the training, I'll learn the task, no matter what it is." And when they've done a task well, reward them with favourable comments like "Daddy feels really good when you help out." You must introduce them to "feeling words" and "feeling statements" because they are in the emotional reasoning phase. Remember always that children (like all of us!) have an inclination towards negative thought, so you never have to tell them how to feel bad, but you do have to help them feel good about something they've done. They need to be encouraged. When they are rewarded or entertained for the day, ask them how they feel about it so they can internalise the good feeling associated with that event. This will help them build a library of good feeling that will sustain them in the future.

10) Are there any historical reasons why, as Irish parents, we are often reluctant to compliment our children?

There are several reasons why historically Irish parents have been reluctant to compliment their children. The history of Ireland is a history of occupation. The Irish were occupied for 700-800 years by people who characterised the native Celts as "dumb and lazy" and as "drunkards and fighters", and they were made to bow their heads or tip their caps to anyone who had any sort of position of authority or any education. If you showed yourself as promising, you were often put down by those in authority because you were getting "above your station." The occupiers were convinced that if you gave the Irish any kind of authority, then their position as governor or occupier would be undermined. If you were working as a servant in one of the Big Houses and you could read or write, that was a disadvantage, because you were getting "above your station." So the "above your station" mentality became a very important factor in the psyche of Irish people. With it came hundreds of years of people not being able to raise their head high, of not being able to concentrate on their own well-being, and it led to parents even encouraging their children not to raise their heads, lest they be hurt or put down. This led to a kind of community despair. Many had to emigrate where some did very well for themselves because they no longer had the suppression of 800 years hanging over them, a suppression that still attaches itself to people today. Many Irish people who travelled did extremely well, while others seemed to have carried that suppression inside them wherever they went. This was especially true of many who went to the UK for labouring jobs. Due to that suppression, as well as loneliness and sadness, many of them did not succeed. But many did do well, so when I talk about Irish men as being "on the shoulders of giants," I'm talking about men who've survived and thrived despite hundreds of years of being subject to the most horrific conditions, not having a real sense of being valued for themselves by either the larger community or even within their own households.

The parents of yesterday felt that children should be seen and not heard, so, as a child, you didn't get to voice what you had to say. And the parents of yesterday had this concern over "swelled heads" – in my 61 years of life, I've yet to see someone who got a swelled head because somebody said something nice about them.

So this whole idea that bragging or boasting about your children in their presence was a bad thing came down through generations of people who were afraid to lift their head above the parapet, who were afraid to see themselves as valuable for themselves. And so long as Irish people had that kind of mentality, the colonisers were able to keep control over them. Nevertheless, I am convinced that as a nation, we are starting to come out of that mentality. We are beginning to see ourselves as we really are and value ourselves and applaud ourselves. We are starting to understand that we have something valuable to offer the world. We're moving away from begrudgery; we're moving away from "Ah sure, I knew him when he had no arse in his pants" or "Ah sure, his father was only a labourer." We're moving away from all the putting people down and the petty jealousies. We're only a generation away from it, but I believe we're moving further and further away from it all the time.

There's a huge generosity in the Irish people, and that's been seen, for instance, in the way that the Irish are always huge givers whenever there's an appeal for people affected by natural disasters. We are a people who've been led a great deal by emotion, and that's a very valuable quality, but if not used wisely, it may become childlike. My view is that the Irish people were never really allowed to grow up so you had generations and generations of children raising children. They had this physical ability to do work and an intellectual ability to write well but emotionally, they were still childlike. They had become stunted in their emotional growth by 800 years of suppression, not having the freedom to express how they really felt. This led them to express themselves through music which was often sad and melancholic, speckled with the occasional cheerful piece.

The modelling for parenting and leadership shown to the Irish people by their occupiers was one of control, control, control. It wasn't a healthy model of relationship that involved neediness being met, and this led Irish parents to be controllers in their homes and Irish bosses to be controllers rather than leaders in the workplace. In addition to this, it led to the lax attitude of the Irish towards the law and law-breaking. For 800 years, people broke the law because it enabled them to laugh behind their hands at the powers-that-be, saying, "You think you're ruling us, but we're shooting your rabbit or killing your deer." There was a celebration of the "cute hoor" – the guy that got away with things – because that type of person becomes a hero under a regime based on suppression. We've grown up with a history of control and law-breaking that still affects Irish relationships today, and this aspect of the Irish character really needs to change.

11) I find my child to be very assertive and outspoken. Is that O.K.?

When your child comes to you and says, "I don't like this" or "I don't like that," you should be applauding yourself, because all children need the ability to say how they feel to an adult without fear. It's a sign that you've given your child that freedom. Most of the people in my generation grew up with a fear of adults; we were told to respect the adults and "respect" was interpreted as "fear." As a result, you never said how felt. You may have gone around the corner and called your mum or dad some awful name, or in your head you may have hoped that something nasty would happen to them, but you never spoke those things out. If a child doesn't speak these things out, they can often start to internalise the feeling that "I'm a bad lad" or "I'm a bad girl" because they know they've been thinking really bad things. Children will often beat themselves up about that later on. On the other hand, if the child SAYS really bad things, something can be done about it, even if the parents don't like to hear what's being said! The words have gone out from the child, and it makes a big difference to how they feel on the inside about themselves. Hopefully, we are producing a people today who are fearless to speak their minds and to act courageously, because they're going out into a world where that's a very important skill. They need to have the capacity to stand up for themselves without fear of being ridiculed or made to feel bad.

12) What makes children "bold"?

"Boldness" is just another method a child has discovered that will help them to get their own way. But what does "boldness" originally mean? I love the word "bold," because the word "bold" means that you are courageous and so when we talk about a bold child, we should be talking about a courageous child. This child is courageous in the sense that he or she has identified a little button in you that can be pressed that will get them their own way in the same way that a pigeon discovers that by tapping on a little sign that it will get them a peanut. It doesn't take an awful lot of time for these patterns to build up. Humans are not a million miles away from Pavlov's dogs, who started salivating when the feeding-time bell was going to ring. We've got to realise that a very large part of us is driven by instinct and conditioning, but that there is a small part of us that can exercise management over those instincts and habits. As humans, we are very susceptible to conditioning. There are people who have been institutionalised who might not be able to open a door, even though they were very functional before they went into the institution. Children analyse the conditions around them and begin to recognise what they can or can't do in order to get their wants met. Think of a screaming baby in the middle of the night. When we parents hear that screaming, we get up and check if they're dry or need food or need burping. So from very early on, the child learns that there are certain activities – certain ways of yelling or screaming or stamping their feet – that get your attention. (In fact, the children of deaf parents don't throw tantrums!) These methods of getting your attention were all survival methods at one stage. Young children would do certain things to get the attention of the adult in order to help them not be at risk or in danger, but we're not in that kind of primitive world anymore. And because we're not in that kind of world, we need to recognise that children are sometimes using those danger signals when all they really want is a hug and to be told that everything is going to be O.K. If you're not picking up on the signals that children are sending to get their emotional NEEDS met, they'll produce an angry response in order to have their WANTS met, wants like sweets or toys or simply to get their own way. And giving in to that child's wants may not be the right thing. We need to comfort our children and to keep reminding them that we are no longer living in prehistoric times. We are living in surroundings that are more comfortable and we don't have to act like cavemen (or cave-children) any more! There are many instincts in us that drive us to act as if we are still in a cave so we've got to be careful of that and understand that a lot of our behaviour is survival behaviour. Survival behaviour causes children to scream and roar to get noticed. If the children are in any way traumatised, then their speaking out to get notice comes from a part of them that's defensive and protecting them. But sometimes they're speaking out just to get something a marketing guru has convinced them that they need.

13) What are your tips for disciplining children when they disobey?

For example, is it o.k. to hit a small child who wouldn't understand verbal reasoning because they've gone out on the road?

When a child goes out on the road, some parents are tempted to hit the child, to teach them that going out on the road is dangerous, but it is much better to remove children from danger than to hit them. Remember: your child doesn't have the library of information that says "That stop sign means stop" or "If I go on the road I may get hit."

You, the parent, are the one that knows those things and you also know that your child, if unattended, will run out on the road. Therefore, if you let your child play on a street where there are passing cars then you're asking for trouble. I used to joke with my mum that because there were so many of us, she used to let us play on the tram tracks! But to return to the issue at hand, I'm saying that children don't know that if they run onto the street, there could be a car coming that could kill them. If a ball goes onto the road, their attention is focused on the ball and the game, not the car. When they're with you on a road or pathway, they need to be contained, but if they do run out onto the road and you hit them for doing it, do you think that will make any difference to the child? No. It will only make them think that you're cruel for hitting them, because they are too young to understand that running out onto the road is a problem. YOU are the one that got a fright, so you wanted to thump them because YOU were scared or upset. THEY weren't scared – they were just doing what a child does. Taking the child from the danger and pointing out to them that going out on the road is dangerous is much more important than the smack, because when you explain the dangers, you're building up a library of information in them and building a caring parent-child relationship. The smack won't keep them from going onto the road in future. By hitting them, you're only building fear into them. If you communicate through fear, they will live fearfully. They'll be afraid to go out onto the road. And that's not good because there should be times when you can go out onto the road. Fear-driven learning is not successful. There are enough fears in us, so we don't need to learn more from our families, particularly from the people who are supposed to be caring for us. Children have a lot of reasoning power as early as two, so two is not too young to explain to them not to go out on the road. In fact, age two is the time when you're trying to impress upon them that your "yes" means "yes" and "no" means "no," so it's a good time to emphasise that going onto the road is a "no-no."

If you want your child to learn about hitting, then hit them. If you don't want them to learn about it, then don't hit them. They're going to get all these knocks and blows from their peers at school so they'll learn all about that type of interaction soon enough. But the big bully adult should not engage in smacking. I think lots of parents would be upset at me saying that, and a case could possibly be made for the gentle tap on the bottom as a little reminder, but beating children into submission is unacceptable. On this island, loads of cases of this type of abuse are coming to light at the moment. When I was growing up, we were slapped by teachers and if we went home and told our parents, we got another slap! And we were told we probably deserved it! We have a generation of adults now who got so many thumps and smacks that they think that's the only way to raise children, but a lot of the people who got punished in this way got deeply scarred by it. Some who got hit like that went too far the other way, however, and are against disciplining children. But disciplining must be done, and the best way is to put a discipline chair somewhere in the house, and say "You must stay there till you apologise or work it out." (It's best to leave them in the chair for a minute per year-of-age, e.g. three minutes for a three-year-old and five minutes for a five-year-old). Children hate to go into those chairs, so, if you start it young, you'll find them saying "Sorry Mummy" or "Sorry Dad" and that's much more effective than the smack. Children don't have a lot of patience but you're the one that must have the patience. You're the one with the 30-40 years of experience who can teach the child the way they should go. Nobody likes to learn in a place where they're bullied, criticised and smacked. If your children are bullied, criticised or smacked at home, will they learn from their parents? No. But if they're treated with love and respect, they will learn at home.

Top 10 Discipline Tips

1. **Be Decisive.** Children's radar picks up the maybe in the no! State it assertively and decisively. Use yes rather then no. For example, "Yes, you can have it when your homework is finished." Delineate tasks for boys. For example, "I would like you to clean your room tonight. That includes putting your clothes away, making your bed, and putting away your toys where they belong."
2. **Be Positive**. Direct attention away from what your child doesn't want to do, to what he does want to do. "As soon as you get out of the bath and brush your teeth, we can read a story."
3. **Explain Yourself.** This promotes the child's reasoning skills. "Hold the knife carefully, cutting away from you, or you'll cut yourself."
4. **Make Rules Impersonal.** Make the conflict between the child and the rule instead of the child and you. Change "I don't want you to drink juice in the living room" to "The rule is: food and drink in the kitchen only, please."
5. **Be Brief and Clear.** When disciplining a child it is not a time to give them a sermon on why you have come up with this philosophy on cleanliness or table manners.
6. **Offer a Choice Whenever Possible.** "You need to have your

room tided up before you go to bed tonight. Do you want to do it now or after dinner?

7. **Reward Good Behaviour.** Give praise, prizes, and hugs for being "caught" doing good! Ask the child for ideas. This is an excellent way to prove you are interested and really listen.

8. **Know When Not to Get Involved.** This will be different for each family, but often it will include school issues and sibling issues. Let a child work out a conflict at school on his own, or resolve a conflict with a sibling without your help.

9. **Work Together**. The effective parent does not say, "Get going" but instead says, "Let's go."
   a. State the problem areas
   b. Ask for suggestions
   c. Come up with a workable approach

10. **Pick Your Battles.** Adjusting expectations may increase cooperation.
    a. Choose your issues. Ask yourself, "Do I really want to set a limit here? Is it important for the child's growth or is it just a personal preference of mine that can be negotiated?"
    b. Is this request age-appropriate? For example, is it reasonable to ask a six-year-old to stop asking questions, or to ask a two-year-old to not request snacks between meals?

14) What's wrong with "spoiling" children?

There's a book I was reading recently about a woman who fed raccoons bread every day. One day she didn't have bread for them, but they didn't understand and all her explanations to them weren't going to make them go away. The raccoons attacked her! And this was the woman who was feeding them every day! This is just like spoiled children. If you keep on giving and giving and giving, they won't act any differently than a wild raccoon. If you don't eventually give them what they want, the child will get mad at you. The woman who fed the raccoons had to move house and stay away for ages, because any time she went back, she was attacked by the raccoons. Don't expect wild animals, no matter how cute, not to behave like wild animals. Our children, no matter how cute, won't have the information naturally that they need to process different situations. We are a little bit above wild animals, though, so children can be taught the proper boundaries. Our children can see, hear and understand both our facial expressions and our verbal expressions, and they know that when we give them an instruction, it's for their own benefit and that this helps them put the new information into their library.

The Biblical statement "Show your children the way they should go" illustrates the importance of being a model to your children. They're looking at you so it's up to you to show them the way they should go. If you go to church and don't force them, but invite them along, they'll want to go. You'll find that children, if not forced, will want to share in your experiences. You can applaud them if they pursue it – that's fine – but showing them is the best thing. Always remember that you are the parent and that

YOU are in charge and not them. There are times they will not want to do what you want to do, but say "I appreciate that you don't want to do what we want to do, but I am responsible for you and I'm in charge, so into the car you go." The child will have a tantrum and kick and scream and roar, but soon it'll be all over. If you give into them and don't do what you think everyone should do, then they feel they can say "no" to everything that you want them to do. You must understand that a child, in their normal defensive mechanism, will not want to do many things. They will therefore do something that they know you don't like. The children have learned the words or actions they can do to make you give in, but don't give in. Say to yourself, "I know they're going to shout and scream and roar but I'm going to strap them into the back seat and take them along. I'll patiently put up with the yelling and screaming. In the past, I might not have put up with it and I might have given in, but now I'm going to press on and not give in and do what's right for all of us."

Children Learn What They Live

If children live with criticism,
They learn to condemn.

If children live with hostility,
They learn to fight.

If children live with ridicule,
They learn to be shy.

If children live with shame,
They learn to be guilty.

If children live with encouragement,
They learn confidence.

If children live with praise,
They learn to appreciate.

If children live with fairness,
They learn justice.

If children live with security,
They learn to have faith.

If children live with approval,
They learn to like themselves.

If children live with acceptance and friendship,
They learn to find love in the world.

Author Unknown

15) Have you got suggestions for teaching children empathy?

We need to get children to understand empathy by relating a given situation to themselves. "Do you know how it hurts when X happens to you? Well, if you do X to your brother, it hurts your brother the same way it hurts you." You teach them empathy rather than allowing them to just think about themselves. Empathy can be learned and it's an emotionally intelligent process. A child's E.Q. (their emotional quotient) can be improved greatly by teaching them emotional skills. As parents, we should put as much effort into encouraging emotional intelligence as we do into intellectual development. The world needs to have people who are balanced – not just academically locked into one way of seeing the world and unable to engage with the emotional side of themselves. If the emotional skills are not learned and encouraged, then people will come to a place where emotionally they have no experience or skills, and it can cause great upset.

Children will always let you know what their needs are. They will show you that they have a need for comfort or attention by making certain noises and gestures. By nature, you are fairly well-equipped to comprehend the different cries or ways in which a child will communicate his or her need for comfort or attention. It's important for parents to react to those sounds and gestures and minister to those needs. The problem with not seeing your child from one day to the next is that you not exposed to those sounds and actions enough to be able to recognise them and act on them, and this can cause awful problems. I believe Bolby was the first to see that children are so easily hurt by separation anxiety because they interpret that when they try to communicate their neediness, their parents don't recognise it. Having intimacy needs met is a crucial backdrop to the development of a child's emotional intelligence.

16) How can we teach our children to express themselves emotionally?

When people come into counselling sessions with me and try to express themselves, they have very few words to express how they're feeling. Those who can't express emotion – in extreme cases – resort to cutting themselves (self-mutilating) or overdosing as a kind of language. I would see all of these behaviours as attempts by people to communicate that something is wrong. Sadly, they don't have sufficient emotional language to communicate this pain in other ways. Some people who come into sessions might use the language "I'm really fucked up right now." That may sound like a nasty word to use, but it's the only word that has any meaning for them. Nevertheless, if you can get someone to express what that means in an emotional way, then you're having success. "I feel uncomfortable... sad... tormented..." There's a huge vocabulary of emotional terms that are so important (some are listed below). Teaching them to your children will help them to convey what's really going on so that they don't have to resort to one big blast like "I hate you" or damaging accusations or words that they'll get punished for using without someone hearing what they're really saying.

Emotions... How do you feel?

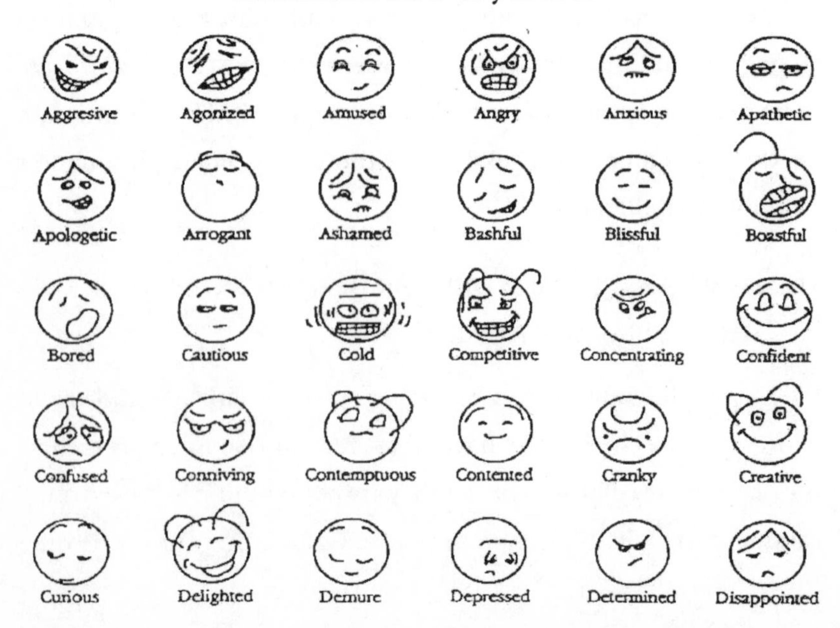

Emotions... How do you feel? – *continued*

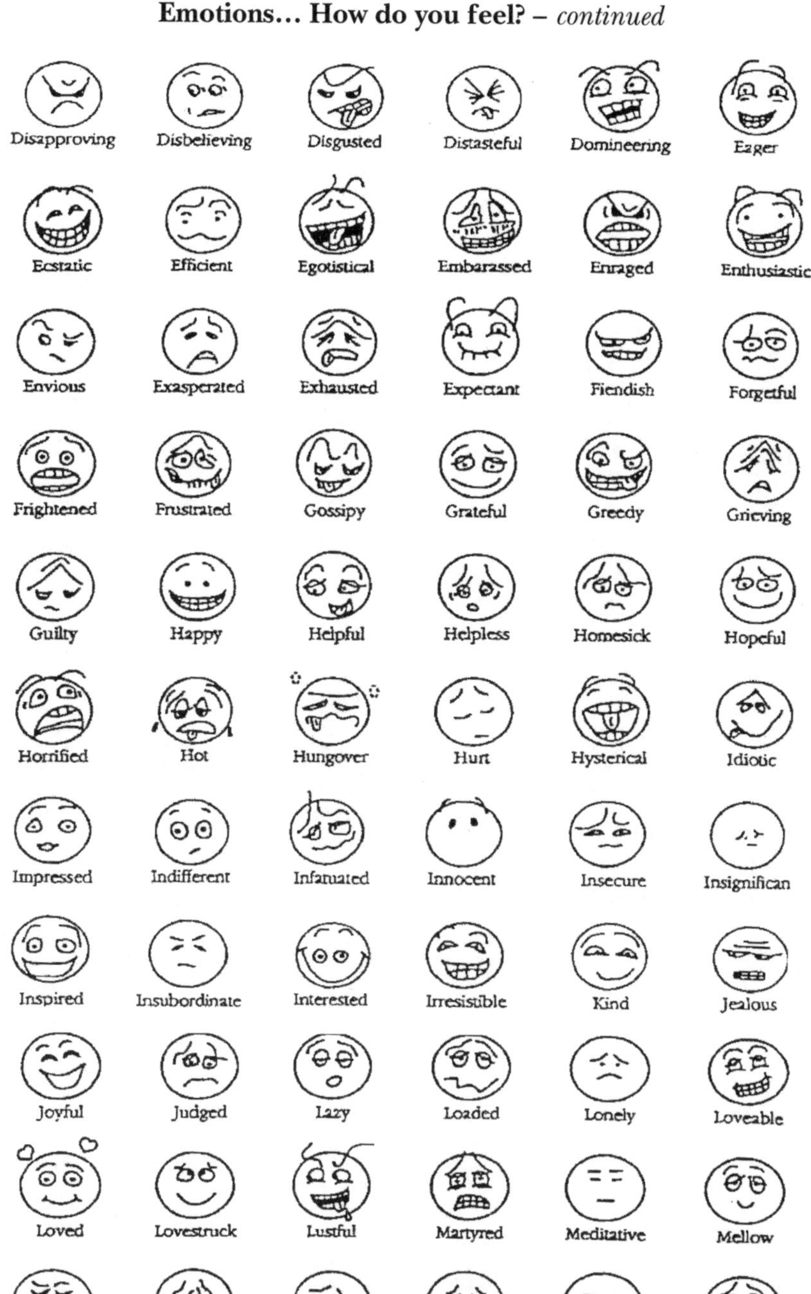

Emotions... How do you feel? – *continued*

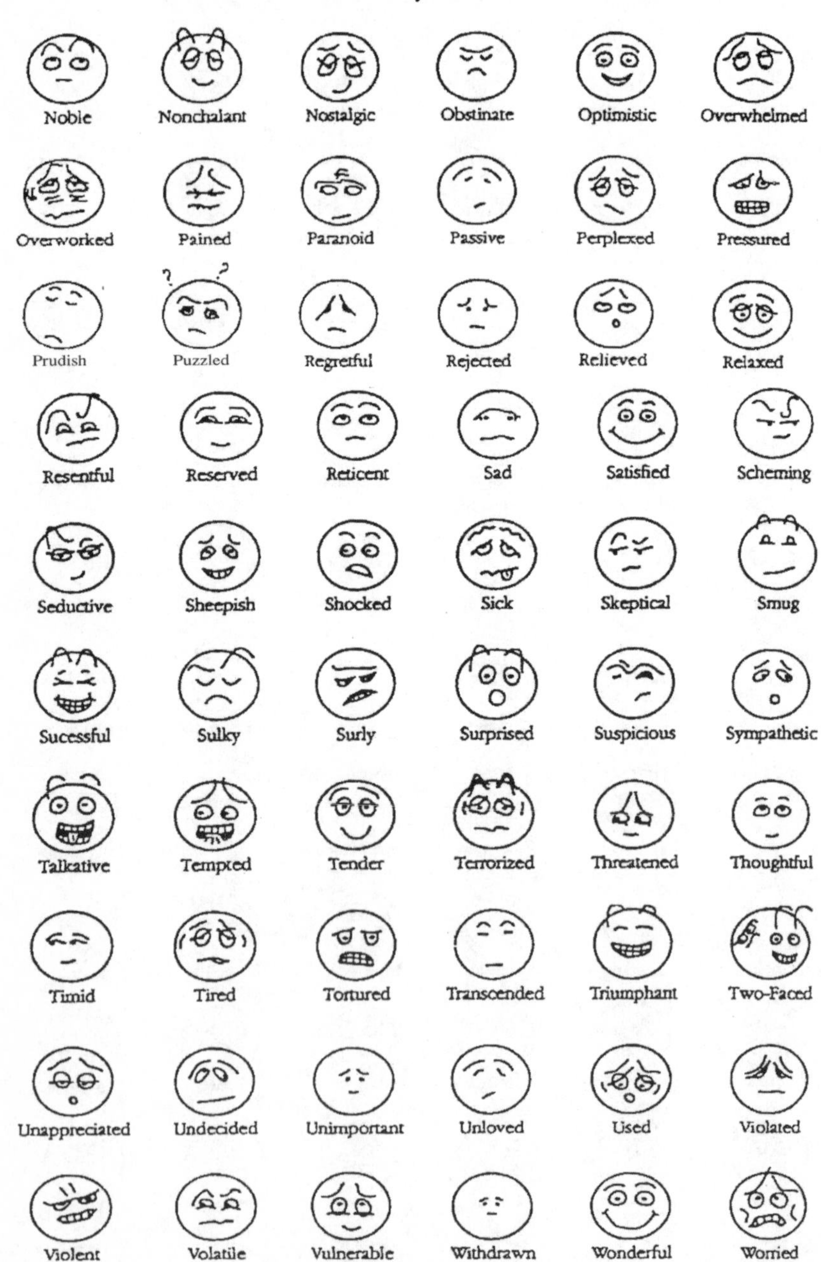

17) Are there especially difficult emotional times for young children as they grow that we need to watch out for?

There are two very difficult times for the child, and they are related to the "crossing over" process that we discussed in Section One. The first difficult time is when the young boy is leaving mum at about eight to go across to dad. The circumstances have to be right for this to occur – he wants desperately to move across to the dad and have that loving relationship. But it's a difficult time because the young boy feels he has to distance himself from his mum as he begins to see things more from dad's view and wants to engage with him. And this time can be very difficult for mum too, because she finds that the little angel who was so compliant and so loving and so wonderful up to a certain point is now dismissing her or ignoring her. She finds that he's not responding to her or to her requests as nicely as he did up until recently, and so she can be quite disappointed in her child at this stage. Similarly, it's also difficult when the little eight-year-old girl is leaving dad to cross over to mum. The little girl will experience many conflicting emotions, while dad will feel very left out. He won't understand why his daughter doesn't want him around so much anymore, and, though it's difficult for all, mum must make the conditions right for the girl to come across.

We will discuss the second difficult time in Section Three, when we discuss parenting teenagers.

18) What are your feelings on bullying, which is such an epidemic in Irish schools at the moment?

To experts, it has become obvious that bullies usually come from the same emotional platform as the bullied. The difference is that these bullies have learned aggressive behaviour as a means of defending their own sensitivity. These young people recognise the vulnerability and sensitivity of other boys or girls because of their own knowledge of that emotional state. In order to end this type of bullying, it is necessary to sit the two children down together and help them understand that they are similar. The bully needs to learn appropriate assertiveness, just as the bullied child needs to learn assertiveness. The situation must be stopped early so that the bullied child doesn't become so harassed that they turn into a bully themselves.

The fact that the bully and the bullied are similar may surprise some, but even as adults we are inclined to dislike the character traits displayed in others that are similar to the ones we hate in ourselves. The trait we dislike in ourselves causes us to be fearful as we struggle to keep it hidden and worry that it will be spotted by others. When we see it in others, it can make us angry towards them and ourselves.

If the intimacy needs discussed previously are met in the early development stages, it will keep children from believing that they have to be aggressive in order to protect themselves. If they feel accepted by you, they will know that their sensitivity is not only accepted by you but valued as well. They will have your reassurance that it's perfectly normal for a child to feel threatened and insecure, and your attention and encouragement will drive these feelings away from the child. Your input will give the child a healthy understanding of his or her own feelings and, as a result, they will have empathy towards others.

19) Have you an opinion on drugs as a treatment for behavioural problems often described as ADD and ADHD?

Pharmaceutical companies are trying to broaden their scope and increase the sale of their medications, especially to children who are neurologically developing. The idea of using SSRIs or medicines like it on the young is, in my opinion, an irresponsible way of approaching behavioural problems in children. I certainly believe we need medical interventions from time to time but there's still not enough information known as to the full extent of the side effects of these drugs, particularly on a developing brain.

In my opinion, ADD and ADHD are heavily promoted by pharmaceutical companies and the books they help finance engage in scare-mongering. Parents react to that, and it's been tremendously damaging. Teachers who are not informed and only see disruptive behaviour in class assume there's been a huge upsurge in ADD or ADHD children, whereas most of these children are actually traumatised and are acting from the defensive side of the brain. If we can get the children to stop acting from that side of the brain, it'll drastically affect their acting out and there won't be a need for this type of medical intervention, which is, in my opinion, just the perceived easy-fix solution.

20) How would you describe dyslexia?

Dyslexia is a term given to people who have difficulty reading or writing because certain neurological connections aren't being made. The child who suffers in this way may be disruptive to get the attention away from their disability. Parents need to watch out for this. Often it's the teacher who first notices the signs. They become suspicious when they see a bright child having problems with reading and writing. This often comes as a surprise to parents because the dyslexic child often demonstrates a real desire for learning. Some signs that teachers and parents pick up on are 1) the child having trouble recognising or spelling words, 2) not being able to structure their essays very well, 3) when spelling, reversing their letters, 4) poor short-term memory causing difficulty with reading comprehension passages or remembering names or recalling certain types of information, 5) poor handwriting, and 6) difficulty writing things off of the board. Dyslexic children often beat themselves up for not being able to do what other children can do.

As a dyslexic myself, I'm very aware that I used to hide my own dyslexia through various methods that I developed. When I was growing up, there was no such word as dyslexia, or if it was around, very few people knew about it. I would have been called lazy or stupid or other terms that are not printable! I couldn't understand why there were so many things I found it easy to do and other things that were very difficult. A big impediment in my own future development was made worse by the fact that my struggle wasn't understood. What I had to look forward to every day at school was getting slapped for spelling words wrong or having difficulty in language classes. Fortunately, I just persisted and believed a little bit more in myself than perhaps other people did, and in time, I was able to overcome the fear around reading or writing, even if I couldn't overcome the dyslexia. I'm still affected by it and have to find other ways to read or write or prepare documentation.

If your child is having trouble writing down what's on the board or reading passages, you really need to examine them just to see if they have some kind of dyslexia and may need help with it. Things are very different from when I was growing up. Schools and parents today commit themselves enthusiastically to the benefit of children with learning disabilities and do enormous work to help them through their struggles. People like Leonardo da Vinci and John F. Kennedy and many other inventors, artists and leaders were dyslexic, so you can reach fame and fortune and make a big impact on the world in spite of these difficulties. Perhaps their learning disability meant that these people could see things in slightly different ways and therefore make a unique contribution.

21) Is it important that our children understand the spiritual world?

Judging by the glut of books and programmes like Harry Potter, The Chronicles of Narnia, and Buffy The Vampire Slayer, it would appear that all children have a fascination with the supernatural. This fascination seems to satisfy their imagination and identifies their need for some form of spiritual understanding. Santa Claus/Christmas, Halloween, and the Easter Bunny have all been forms used to help satisfy the inner desire of the child to have its spiritual need met. Some families introduce their children to a God who is fearful and punishing, and others introduce their children to a God who is all-loving and forgiving. Either way, the child's image of God will be formed more by the way they see you and how you interact or engage with them, because you are, in effect, their "God" until they get a little older and find their own. There is evidence to suggest that children who are introduced to the moral teachings of their church fair better than children who have had no spiritual input. If you think about it, most of the laws that are in the western world are based on the morality laws found in most religions of the world, and have been successful in maintaining a form of order and civil justice. Also, the idea of a child understanding the possibility of a power greater than themselves satisfies their hunger for the supernatural and at the same time allows them somewhere to go when they're alone and feel there's nobody there for them. As the old adage says, "There are no atheists in a fox hole." The idea of crying out to God in a crisis is universal, and children need their fears to be met with hope (as we all do!).

When your children engage with any sort of spiritual experience or have a fascination for the supernatural, it is important that you converse with them and present your adult view to them. Their limited library of information about spirituality needs topping up and the best person to instruct the child in the spiritual world is the parent. Also, it's important that parents don't assume that their children understand everything that they are watching. They do not take in or see everything that they are watching in the way that you do. Therefore, it is important, when watching any programme or film or reading any book (whatever its content), that you take it as an opportunity for dialogue with your child.

SECTION THREE

the teenager

1) SHOULD WE BEGIN TO TREAT OUR CHILDREN DIFFERENTLY ONCE THEY'VE BECOME TEENAGERS?

When our children enter their teens and are finally able to look out for themselves, it is very important that we mark that coming-of-age in their lives. One of the things that I have huge issues with in our society is that we don't have a coming-of-age ceremony that allows men and women to become grown up – they often remain in the prince and princess state and never really become kings and queens. They never get this new announcement that says, "Blessed are you; you're the new man or woman on the block," unlike what you might find with the young males and females in the Jewish culture. Young Jewish males, at 12 years of age, have a Bar Mitzvah in which they go through a ritualistic coming-of-age that allows them to participate with the men. They are now free to leave their mums and join together with men where they are LISTENED to. The principle behind that, of course, is that they have something to say and that the men want to hear it. And with a Bat Mitzvah, which is the same thing for the females, young Jewish woman have the opportunity to have a closer relationship with the women and to engage in womanly work and learn womanly ways. There needs to be some ritualistic coming-of-age, so my advice to fathers is to make one up in your own household. When young men come into puberty and have their first wet dream, I often suggest that their fathers, if they have a close enough relationship with their sons, should explain that they are now producing sperm so they are in a position to be seen as "coming-of-age." They are changing – there is an elongation of their physical self and they are becoming more man-like. To mark that, there should be a celebration, and, similarly, there should also be a celebration when a young girl has her first period.

This ritualistic coming-of-age should occur at 13 or so, so that we begin preparing them for 16-17 years of age when they will be in a position to leave mum and dad emotionally and take responsibility for themselves, having been equipped by mum and dad to do so. The loving and comforting of the father and the mother, which was the parents' responsibility up to that point, is an investment that the young adult must take and use for themselves as they move into the future. They must realise that this investment of love from their parents is an essential building block that they will use as they go out to enjoy the world in a healthy way.

2) When does adolescence begin and end?

Adolescence is a term that was only introduced in the 1900s, and before that, there was no such thing as an adolescent. What you had was a boy or a man, or a girl or a woman. There was no "in-between" time. I think that adolescence was a convenient term given to children when they prolonged their staying at home or going to school. Unfortunately, this title has given young men and women a sort of license to behave badly or immaturely. In my opinion, the term "adolescent" should never be used, as it isn't a useful term for young men and women. Boys and girls reach maturity at a certain time and that's when you should start treating them with a different type of respect and giving them extra responsibilities. There are many societies where young men and women, when they reach this stage of maturity, become full-time contributors to the financial requirements of the home. And they're not seen to be any less than man or woman. In our Western society, where young people are given more opportunity for academic study, we have decided to give them a label that allows them not to mature in certain ways, and that's not right.

When young teenagers start to have the 800% increase in estrogen or testosterone roaring through their systems, it has a profound effect on their thinking, their reasoning, and their emotional state. However, the more you show you understand them – since you have been there and done that and have the T-shirt – the more you're able to comfort them in their struggles and the more you're able to respect the difficulties they encounter as they handle the new responsibilities that you've given them. Treating them with this type of respect will give them greater maturity as they move towards that age of independence (16-17 years of age).

An important thing to remember is that when they come at you flaring with anger or upset, your best approach is to ask them what's hurting. That usually knocks the wind out of their sails, and shows that you care about what's going on inside of them.

Also, some mothers worry about their sons grunting responses to their questions. It's not dissimilar to the responses they often get from their husbands, as men are not that inclined to engage in long conversations. Expect your sons to be similar.

3) WHAT DO YOU THINK I SHOULD DO ABOUT THE FACT THAT MY TEENAGER HAS A VERY BLACK-AND-WHITE, "STORM THE BARRICADES" VIEW OF POLITICS AND THE WORLD?

Young adults, from about the age of 14 or 15, see things in black and white and don't really engage with the grey way of thinking. It's either right or wrong, and that is why they are more likely to become involved in cults or become involved with SAVE THE WHALES or other big causes. For those of us who have misplaced our idealism, they can highlight perspectives that we've wrongly left behind, especially those of us who've moved from a hippy state with the flairs and the long hair to the suit and the short hair! They want to see positive change through politics, and they are deeply concerned with pollution and how we treat the earth. It's not a bad thing that they go through this stage and it's not bad that they express these sentiments at this time. Just remember that their understanding is based on a narrowness of viewpoint. As they get older, they'll get a greater understanding of the way the world works. This black and white storm-the-barricades attitude usually lasts till about 22 or 23. The speed with which they are able to come out of the black-and-white thinking is linked to how well-nurtured they were during the emotional reasoning period of development (up to ten years of age).

This storm-the-barricades period is a fairly hectic time for the family, but it's just another healthy development stage and we have a responsibility to be there as confidants and wisdom-givers when they come to us with these kind of ideas. We need to be there to understand them and give them support rather than be critical of them.

4) Are there especially difficult times for teenagers that we need to watch out for?

As we've already mentioned, there are two very difficult times for the child, and they are both related to the "crossing over" process. The first difficult time is when the child is about eight and attempts to cross over from the opposite-gender parent to the same-gender parent. The other difficult time is when the child reaches about 16-17 and wants to leave mum and dad and have his or her independence. Now, if you understand that this is a development stage that's part of a normal process, you'll be feeling calmer, having already spoken to him or her about it and standing by. You and the child are prepared for it, so that when he or she does feel these feelings, it's not such a big tug-o-war, a battle of wits, a "them and us" situation. It's a very healthy transition. It's important for a young man or woman of this age to feel "I can now set out on my own and start a new tribe or my own kingdom," because that's what independence is all about – moving away to start a new tribe or a new kingdom.

5) In your opinion, is it wrong want your kids to have the experiences that you didn't have yourself?

A difficult childhood can cause us as parents to make internal promises about how we will raise our own children. We may say to ourselves, "My father never let me stay out late, so I will always let my son stay out till all hours." These internal promises may come from a good motive, but they can have disastrous results. The situation when you were growing up was very different from life today. And if you try to apply those old ideas and ideals in this time and place, you'll be making very unwise choices. For example, if a mother decides she won't take a certain action because she made a promise to herself that she wouldn't based on her own childhood, that may be a huge disadvantage for the child. All children need security, and believe it or not, children who are not receiving security in the form of safe boundaries and limits feel alone and uncared for. What's more, your child will not even appreciate it when you're giving them something that you never had, because they probably don't even want it! Here's an example: a friend of mine's dad was a workaholic and was never around. As a small boy, my friend decided, "I will always bring my son for a walk on Saturday afternoons," because that's what he would have loved his father to do with him when he was a boy. When my friend finally had a son of his own, he did exactly as he always swore to do: he sacrificed lucrative overtime hours at his work in order to go for walks with his son every Saturday. Sadly, his son hated and resented the walks. On a Saturday afternoon, all he wanted to do was play football with his friends but he never could due to these walks with his father. He grew more and more angry towards his dad and more and more distant. He thought of his father as a spoilsport for taking him on the walks and by the time my friend was terminally ill with cancer, their relationship had deteriorated badly. I was able to explain to his son that his grandfather had been very distant and that it was out of that childhood hurt that his dad had insisted on the walks. When the son understood, he and my friend were able to reconcile, but as you can see, the internal promise that my friend made with himself based on his own childhood neglect badly affected his own relationship with his son. Why are such internal promises dangerous and always bad? Because they interfere with our ability to act in the moment. My friend should have involved himself in his son's interest in football and been more sensitive to the fact that the walks came at a time that was socially awkward for his son. He should have figured out ways in which his son wanted to bond with him and not dragged his own son out for walks just because that's what he would have liked as a boy.

6) Do you consider it wrong to push our children to succeed at something we always wanted to be good at?

A man or woman will often have a view of how their child should be, and that is often based on what they always aspired to but didn't achieve. As a result, they try to influence their child in a particular direction. It's very important that you put in the bin all your ideas about how your child should be, because your child is completely unique, a 400 million to one chance in a world very different from the one you were born into. They might not have any of the character traits that you have or the physical strength that you have, or the appearance or other qualities that you have. They have their own qualities, strengths and abilities, and to know them intimately helps you to give them support in the direction they are going or should be going. Encourage them in the area they'd be best at, rather than forcing them into an area where you yourself haven't achieved. That's especially dangerous to do, because you'll find that children want to support their parents' ideas and want to be what you want them to be – because they don't see any other way – and they'll often forsake what might be their best opportunities in order to please their mother and father. And you'll often find that they later regret having gone that way, because they had forsaken their own talents and interests.

I was passionate about rugby as a young man and wanted my own sons to be good rugby players, hoping that one day they might run out in a green jersey for Ireland. My two boys went to a rugby school and the eldest boy was very committed to playing the game. But the boys also had a desire to study music. My attitude towards music was not very positive, as so many members of our family had been in the music industry and had not fared well financially in that endeavour. Because of this, I insisted that they concentrate on the rugby, until one day I got a phone call to my office informing me that my eldest boy was in hospital with a suspected broken back. I stood over the cot looking down at my son and made a promise that if he came out of that intact, he could play all the music that he wanted and he didn't have to live my dream. Thankfully he recovered and whereas he continued to love rugby, he made music his priority, at which he has showed great talent and ability.

7) ARE THE YOUNG PEOPLE WE SEE AIMLESSLY/AGGRESSIVELY ROAMING THE STREETS DEMONSTRATING THE KIND OF ASSERTIVE "FEARLESSNESS" THAT YOU WERE EXTOLLING IN SECTION TWO?

We must take time to consider a type of fearlessness that we see in certain young people today, which is very different than the "can-do" fearlessness we want to inspire in our children. Take a young man who has not been heard or listened to, one who has had difficulties in school that were not appropriately understood – difficulties that may have been caused by having an alcoholic or drug-addicted mother or father. He leaves school – or is forced out – and is now out on the streets trying to make something for himself. He's very limited intellectually because his academic facility was taken away from him – due to his lack of concentration or other problems – and he's a developing young man so he's physically like a feral cat or anything that's wild. And yet he has to survive – and remember: one of the reasons he's alive today is because there's enough genetic makeup in him that enabled his people to survive in the first place. So now, as he tries to survive in the world with very limited resources, he may fearlessly use means that the majority of the population would consider dangerous or wrong. He may take easier ways out since he's more subject to being easily led, but he needs to survive, and young men and women like him will do what they have to in order to survive and the ways that they do so may be very different from what most would consider normal.

Many of these guys are really super kids and very sensitive, but they can't afford to let that aspect of themselves be visible in the struggle to survive. To deal with that struggle, they use drugs and alcohol to suppress their sensitivity or entertain a kind of fearlessness or fierceness that helps them get on in the world. But that's just a survival instinct and is very different from the assertiveness we're trying to encourage in our children.

8) SHOULD WE BE WORRIED ABOUT THE COMPANY OUR CHILD KEEPS?

There is only a need for parents to worry about the company their child is keeping if they haven't gotten to know their child well in the first place. If you know your child, they'll know what you value and they'll be sound young men and women. And it won't matter what type of area you're living in. If you're giving them a real sense of can-do, that sense will help them to make wise decisions and will give them opportunities they wouldn't otherwise have gotten.

Let me go one step further and say that if you don't know your child, then you shouldn't be giving them any advice! If you don't know that child and that child doesn't know you, and that child is doing things to make life difficult for themselves as a teenager by starting their own tribe, then maybe it's because they're trying to get out of the relationship with you because you never got to know them and it's all too painful. What you need to understand is that by knowing them intimately and by promoting them as people and offering them, at the earliest opportunity, responsibilities carefully balanced with freedom, you're helping them in a way that means, when they are 16 or 17, they're less likely to make bad or self-destructive decisions. They're less likely to make the kind of move that might jeopardise their career, etc. Also, if you are intimate with your child and know them well and they are still considering a big decision at that age, you'll know that they are wise enough to do what others might not be able to do at that age.

Take a moment to listen today
To what your children are trying to say
Listen today whatever you do
Or they won't be there to listen to you

Listen to their problems
Listen to their needs
Praise their smallest triumphs
Praise their smallest deeds

Tolerate their chatter
Amplify their laughter
Find out what's the matter
Find out what they're after

But tell them that you love them every single night
And though you scold them be sure you gold them
Tell them everything is alright, Tomorrow's looking bright

Author Unknown

SECTION FOUR

parenting today

There are many issues facing Irish parents today that have never faced us before. In this section, we will look at some of these issues and see how we might overcome these new challenges.

1) HAVE YOU FOUND THAT BOTH PARENTS WORKING FULLTIME HAS A NEGATIVE EFFECT ON THE CHILDREN'S EMOTIONAL DEVELOPMENT?

There's nothing wrong with both parents working, but if you're looking at best practice, then I would suggest that for the first three years of a child's life, that a parent, preferably the nurturer – the mother – stays home. It's important that they have some level of continuity or sense of connection, especially with the mother, during that time. And the reason I'm saying that is that I don't believe we are developed enough during those nine months in the womb. The three years after the birth is really an extension of the mother-child connection that we see in the womb, and this "outer womb" period is also an extension of the period of development that began in the womb. The successful survival of the child is greatly helped by maintaining a close relationship with the mother during those first three years. It's as if a woman actually carries her child for three years and nine months – that's how long it takes before the child starts to recognise itself as separate from the mother and is able to really branch out on its own.

Children at four, having just come out of that womb phase, are really too young to go to school. Yes, they can be somewhere where there is play going on and even play which contains an educational subtext, but to start formal schooling at four is, in my view, a mistake. By six or seven, they are much better able to cope with the more scholastic side of school.

Going into the future, we don't know what damage will arise from children being dropped off at a crèche at seven in the morning and being collected at seven in the evening. Perhaps it will only result in the child coming up with a different coping mechanism to deal with that situation and perpetuate its survival. In Ireland, it's a relatively new phenomenon and we're just making it up as we go along. We've been here on earth a long, long time, and over thousands of years we've had to adapt and change to suit each change in our environment. The children born into the world today will adjust accordingly to enable the human race to survive, because survival is the brain's priority.

2) What advice can you give to parents who are away from their children a lot and may feel guilty about it?

We have to be encouraged in knowing that the vast majority of people are doing the right thing with regards to the raising of their children. But there are a minority of people who are struggling, because due to work, separation or divorce, they feel guilty about leaving their children and are compensating in unhealthy ways. The guilt that women feel in these cases is actually the innate feeling that a woman will always feel when she has to leave her children – it's a part of her design, a design factor common in all women. Men and women in these situations fear that they are not giving their children what they need so they try to over-compensate by making their children "happy" all the time and by doing everything for them when they are together. To these parents, happiness is when they see the children smiling or laughing, and they get very hurt and very saddened themselves when they see their children crying or getting upset. We are all moved when we see our children upset, but we have to understand that the way to deal with such a situation isn't giving them more gifts so that they are happy and smiling temporarily. We have to comfort them. It's a big problem when the adult lacks the ability to comfort the child and to know that what that child needs at that sad moment is really a hug or an arm around them and an assurance that everything is going to be OK. If children are only given "treats" in those situations, they get into the place of "wanting" and lose touch with their real needs. They'll want another toy or they'll want another hour up at night or they'll want to watch the television for longer; they'll want a Playstation or an X-Box or whatever else is going, and you'll be under pressure to provide that. Then you have a short-term smiley, happy kind of appearance in the children, but in the long-term what you're doing is winning some little, minor battles but losing the war. You might say that we shouldn't see our relationship with our children as warlike but in actual fact it is that kind of relationship – it will always be a “them and us” situation. They are determined to get their way, and in many ways, because of our guilt or the circumstances of our past, we want to let them. But in that case, what we are actually saying to our child is “You really are the Boss in the house; you’re the one that’s in control.” What many adults don’t understand is that when you give that type of management over to the child, you’re looking for them to manage you and the world around them with very little information to go on. Their own library of information is limited to a whole series of wants, and they won’t necessarily know what they need. It leads to them being very confused, and these confused children are then likely to act out in bad behaviour, because their bad behaviour is the result of expecting things to be done the way they want. Selfishness, aggressiveness, not wanting to do work at school, only doing work for teachers they like, etc. are all the consequence of this type of situation. And so what we have is a generation of people growing up with that selfish outlook, who will not survive in the world. Now sadly, in all circumstances where you have that kind of rot, when you put it into the barrel of the world, it spreads. And you’re getting more and more people who have that type of attitude – that the child should take authority. I have an issue with the Charter of Rights of Children because it focuses solely on rights. I fully agree that children need to have their rights acknowledged as a protection, but rights without responsibilities is a kind of a nonsense. And, when it comes to very specific rights, you can’t really put together a comprehensive package that covers all children, because they all have different personalities and live in different circumstances.

Experts tell us correctly that every one of your children will be uniquely different and that you are the most important person in their lives. If you, as the one that is best able to deal with their issues, hand it over to the United Nations or any other body to set down a particular Bill of Rights, I think you're making a dreadful mistake. And when the ISPCC and others attempt to enforce some of these rights without responsibilities, they are actually promoting a situation in which the child actually does call the shots. Give the ammunition to a child without them having the full library of information, and they are likely to kill you; they are likely to give you the chop, because that's the way they are. These are strong statements to make but children are parasitic. They live off of you in order that that they might survive, and if that happens without some kind of management, you, as a parent, are letting them become parasites on the rest of the world. They will grow to think that the world owes them something then rather than that they have something to contribute to make the world a better place.

3) What can be done about the increasingly rampant problem of childhood obesity?

As you have certainly read, there is a connection between childhood obesity and numerous health problems, including juvenile diabetes. In some cases, children are becoming overweight because their food intake is too large when they are very young – in other words, they are being over-indulged. If children are forced to eat large amounts of food when they're younger, their bodies become accustomed to large portions that are not used up as fuel. When combined with little or no exercise, all the body does is to store up fat with the objective of having stores in case of famine, a leftover survival mechanism from earlier times. What needs to happen is that parents should be giving sensible amounts of food to their children. You know the food appropriate to the age and size of the individual child, and, if you don't, you should take the time to learn. You should also acquaint yourself with the nutritional value of various foods. Children need a balanced diet that meets their nutritional needs, as opposed to what's most convenient on a busy week night.

4) WHAT RECOMMENDATIONS DO YOU HAVE FOR FAMILIES WITH REGARD TO THEIR MEAL TIMES?

Remember that just as you may be focusing too much on convenience because you're knackered after work, your child will also prefer the faster, more convenient foods because they want to get back to playing, etc. That is not the best thing for them or for you, however. My suggestion is that at least once a day, if at all possible, you and your children should sit around the table and have a meal together as a family. I think that one of the biggest disasters in family life today is that families don't sit down to eat together. Children often don't see you eating and therefore don't see normal table manners or behaviours that are appropriate around a table. They also don't get the chance to engage with members of their own family in conversation around the table. Family meals are a very good place where people can share what's happening with their lives, how school has been, what difficulties have arisen, etc. Sitting around the table is almost like praying together – "When you eat together, you meet together" – and if you meet together, there's a fair chance that you'll start talking about where you're at. Once again, it's up to the parent and not the child to insist on such an arrangement. If the parent makes the time for such a commitment, the benefits are huge for the children in the long run. If you don't do it, the child will want to take the fastest food they can get, so they can get back to the television or get back to the X-Box or whatever else they're playing with at the time. They're going to go for chicken nuggets and chips or a burger or some takeout, because they can just sit down and eat it as they do some non-bonding activity.

These days, children get very used to the idea of speed-eating while watching television or engaging in some other activity, but, while the digestive system is very well designed, it is also very delicate, so it's not a good idea for the children to be occupied with some kind of television programme or video game when they're eating food. It's not healthy, because it doesn't allow your digestive system to deal with food properly and distribute the energy that is required for your body from that food. When they're shovelling stuff into their stomachs, their stomach won't necessarily understand that it's engaging with a food activity. It thinks the child is engaged with watching television or playing a video game. Parents should try to understand this and try as much as possible to not have that kind of thing happen.

While it is very important for families to eat together and engage in discussion with one another while they do so, it is very important that you teach your children not to speak with their mouths full. If you speak while you're eating, the little trap door that separates the lungs from the stomach is waving back and forth and it makes the possibility of choking much more likely. People who have choked on their food in restaurants usually did so because they had a mouthful of food but kept jabbering away and the food went down the wrong way. So, again, just remind your children of the very sensible old saying: "Don't speak with your mouth full." Is this being taught to children today? I think not. These days we often have conversations with people who are chatting away with their mouth full. You say something and they're speaking back to you with a whole lot of blah, blah, blah... Although it's great to hear what somebody has to say, they're putting themselves at risk.

There are psychologists working with food companies, toy manufacturers and marketing people, and they are very well aware of how children respond to things, so they help these companies deliberately target their products at children. I often have issues with members of my own profession who use their knowledge of the demands and feelings that children have for this purpose. In the case of the food industry, it works like this: Because parents feed their children a lot of sweet items or salty items very early on in life, experts have realised that children have an automatic attraction to very sweet foods and to high levels of salt. The food companies hear this and say, "Children's taste buds are excited by the kind of foods that were given to them as infants that contained high levels of sugar and salt. What we must do is to stimulate that memory." They add sugar and/or salt to their foods, regardless of the fact that it makes the food unhealthy. As for the toy companies, many have caught on to what their marketing people have said, which is that the way to win it is to sell to children because the guilty mums and dads will buy them whatever they want.

5) In your view, what are some of the difficulties facing mixed-culture families?

In this country we are going to have more and more mixed-culture families, and no culture should be made out to be better or worse than another. That's a very dreadful thing to do. I have a Palestinian client who was born in Jerusalem, and she has lived elsewhere for much of her life. When asked where she is from, she will never say Jerusalem, but always another part of the Middle East. She would not say she was Palestinian because people would form immediate opinions, but I say to her, "Why not proudly say you were born in Jerusalem? Many people would be happy to hear that. You need to value where you were born. You are part of a nation of people – the Palestinians. If you don't embrace that, you'll be forever ducking and diving and pretending you're someone else. And that will not help you in the long run. If you don't embrace your own culture, you'll regard other cultures as better than yours and you'll do damage to yourself." So if your parents are two different colours or cultures, be proud. If your Dad's Nigerian and you're mum's Irish, be proud. You've brought another kind of gifting and another valuable genetic make-up into the country. We all need to feel proud and rooted and connected to our ancestors. It doesn't matter if your parents were working class or from a difficult cultural situation. What matters is that you're proud of them, because they caused you to be here today. They are the product of generations and generations of survivors. Under slightly different circumstances, they might have been very rich (or very poor). You should not be dismissive of them. That's the wrong attitude to take towards culture or class or place of origin. It's something we all need to look at, and it's a parental responsibility to speak well of your parents and grandparents. Your child doesn't know that your Grandad was a brute. Why feed them with stuff that's not necessary? There must have been things about him that were encouraging. You personally have to deal with the issues related to your mother and father, but you don't need to put the sins of the father upon the heads of the children or grandchildren. That forgiveness is your business, not theirs. It's important for children to associate with grandparents or aunts and uncles. Never go into a dismissive mode about where they're coming from or what their background is. You want the child to go on and live healthily. Also, there are cases where children are told about their auntie Mary – "She was odd" – and then someone will say to the child "You're just like Mary", and the child starts to fear they'll be odd. That's a very unfair thing to put upon a child. They're their own person. They are uniquely themselves and they really don't need to worry about some trait that is perceived to be inherited.

6) How can we help our children have regard for people from other cultures and backgrounds?

Humans are very tribal and love to think "My tribe is better than your tribe" and "My street is better than your street." And this kind of thinking is often related to economic status. People these days are often boasting about the fact that they live in nicer houses or send their children to a paid school instead of a state school. This is really quite ridiculous but is probably so rampant here because for 800 years, the people of Ireland were subjects rather than citizens, and, as subjects rather than citizens, we had authorities over us that made us feel like we were down and unimportant, no matter what tribe we came from. In the last 90 years, we've gained some level of independence and have a Constitution that protects our rights, but many of us are still holding on to that old ruling class idea based on wealth or education. As citizens of the state, we shouldn't be focused on ruling classes. We should merely say, "There go I but for the grace of God." Given slightly different circumstances, all of us could be living in a mansion or a council house.

We need to teach our children the values of equality and humility. If you go down Sheriff Street, the young people aren't particularly happy working with the people in Dorset Street. They keep very much to themselves, because they see their place as being better and more important. The more impoverished different places around the city become, the more tribal and closely guarded they become, and they live like that because they don't have financial clout to escape from those areas. The same happens for the very rich. They close up their gates and have more security and only keep certain company. We all need to develop the ability to move between different castes or tribes, and the way to do that is by getting to know each other and be less fearful of each other.

7) Can you describe some of the problems facing blended families or families affected by divorce or separation?

Whether you're the father in a blended family or a divorced family or a part-time dad, you still have to understand that you have a role. You are a survivor. You have in you a lot of learning and experiences that you can pass on. You have a huge library of information about how the world works, so the more information that you can pass on to the children who've been put into your care, the more beneficial it will be for future generations. You can help your children understand why you want them to get on and develop their different talents and abilities. And you can help them get out of difficulties they might be experiencing. In particular, the more you know about the ways in which separation or divorce may be affecting the child, the better you'll be able to deal with the situation. The adult population has to be educated about how certain circumstances are affecting our children emotionally. We will not see a reverse of divorce or abortion or contraception in our time because of the way in which they're drawn into the western world, so we shouldn't just say "I wish it was the way it was…" We must say, "This is the day" that we've been given and work around this age to the best benefit for our children.

Divorce or separation causes most children to feel insecure and regularly upset. That said, I'm sure there are cases of children who have thrived after divorce or separation because the circumstances in the marriage were so extreme, so there's no wholesale judgment that can be made about how divorce or separation affects children. The vast majority of cases are not extreme, and some of these marriages could still be worked out. One expert from the United States, Judith S. Wallerstein, who's quoted in most studies on divorce and separation decided to write a book about good marriages, because in her studies she realised that there wasn't a great deal of difference between families that stayed together and those that broke up. Looking at them from the outside, you couldn't tell which marriage between two was the happy one – they both faced and regularly dealt with the same problems. The difference was commitment. The commitment wasn't there in the case of the ones that fell apart. The "happy" ones were the ones where the people stuck it out, because no marriage or person is happy all the time. French scientists have determined that attraction is triggered by a chemical reaction at the start of a relationship that lasts six to twelve months, but after that high goes, commitment is needed. It's a wonderful means of bringing people together but this blind love will not continue so we must commit to one another. This chemical reaction is yet another survival mechanism. The reason we survive as a species is that it encourages us to engage us with other humans in such a blinded way, and procreation ensues.

Once you've committed to your partner, that love feeling will re-emerge from time to time. But that will never happen unless you are committed to that person through thick and thin. You'll fall in love with the same person over and over again, but you have to be willing to stay in for the long haul. If you say, "I'll fall in love over and over again with different people and have that buzz again and again for the rest of my life," you'll never find true love, because that is a very selfish approach. I fear that children being raised today to be happy-clappy all the time, whose parents never let them be sad or dissatisfied (or even pause for reflection) will never be able to maintain the type of commitment that a good marriage requires.

8) What are some of the problems that the parents of adopted children can face?

Believe it or not, fathers of adopted children fare very well – more so than the mothers – particularly if the adopted child is a daughter because a girl looks to bond with a man, even if it's not her natural father. She'll still be attracted towards him during that flirtatious time that a daughter has towards her daddy. The danger often is not with the dad but with the mother, because the child is missing the signature scent of its birth mother. When adopted boys are initially difficult, it's usually to do with the trauma of adoption. The trauma of adoption can trigger the defensive mechanism of the brain in the child, because it has been separated from its natural mother. They imagine that something terrible is going to happen all the time. They can become hyper-vigilant and fearful and, in some cases, paranoid. Even if they have the most loving parents caring for them, they are still in defensive mode and can therefore be a handful. As you know, I have described this as "infantile post-traumatic stress disorder" (iPTSD), and I think it's very prevalent in a lot of these children who are adopted. Mothers and fathers need to understand that this is a likely occurrence in adopted children or any children who may have experienced trauma before the age of three, and if it does show itself, they need to seek professional help. The child wants to be loved and reach out to these people but can't. The parents are very loving and can't understand why the child is so defensive or upset, so they need to understand this as well. The children often develop phobias or imaginary illnesses to get the kind of attention they need. It's a very traumatic and sad time for the child who lives in that world, but they just need a bit of professional help to free them from this condition.

conclusion

During the writing of this book, I was aware that some people would be infuriated and others happy by the things I have to say about us as a species. Those controversies aside, I hope that you have learned much and that you have taken away the idea that, even if every book in every library were filled with praise for our ancestors, enough could never be said about those great survivors. I am confident, no matter what we do, no matter what our children are exposed to – be it painful suffering or other extreme hardship – the ones who have gone before us have left us a legacy of survival by their heroic endeavour and resilience. They have set the scene by improving the already flexible and able human being. They are the Giants on whose Shoulders we are Standing, enabling us to see further.

APPENDIX ONE

childhood questionnaire

Drawing from your memories of childhood, list one word or one phrase descriptions for each of your parents (both strengths and weaknesses).

FATHER

Strengths
(For example, hard working, easy to talk to, honest)

____
____
____
____

Weaknesses
(for example, lots of anger perfectionistic, rigid)

____
____
____
____

MOTHER

Strengths

____
____
____
____

Weaknesses

____
____
____
____

What things did you most like about yourself when you were a child? *(For instance, I liked that I was so creative. I liked being the best swimmer in my neighbourhood. I liked the way I could talk easily with adults)* ______________________________

____

____

What things did you like least about yourself when you were a child? *(For instance, I felt like a klutz around my friends. I was afraid to stand up for myself. I didn't get good grades like the other children)*

____

____

____

When you were a child, how would Mum:
Praise you? ______________________________
Criticise you? ____________________________
When you were a child, how would Dad:
Praise you? ______________________________
Criticise you? ____________________________
As you grew up, how did you know Mum loved you? *(For instance, she would hug me and tell me she loved me)* ________________

____

As you grew up, how did you know that Dad loved you? *(For instance, he would buy me things – clothes and toys and stuff)*

____

How did Mum and Dad deal with conflict between themselves?
Dad would ______________________________
Mum would ______________________________
How did Mum and Dad handle conflict with you?
Dad would ______________________________
Mum would ______________________________
How did you know your parents loved each other as you were growing up? How did they show it? *(For instance, they hugged and kissed a lot. They spoke kindly to each other. They laughed a lot together)*

____

Indicate either 'Mum' or 'Dad', 'both' or 'neither' next to the following phrases to help describe your home life as a child
Family leader ____________________________
Main disciplinarian ________________________
Quick temper ____________________________
Comfortable giving affection to me ________________
Hard to please ____________________________
Parent I felt closest to ______________________

APPENDIX TWO

removing the lies

ACCEPTANCE / FORGIVENESS

I FORGIVE MYSELF FOR BELIEVING THE LIE THAT I WAS LOVED CONDITIONALLY.

THIS MADE ME FEAR REJECTION. IT ALSO CAUSED ME TO BE A PEOPLE PLEASER, A HAVE-TO PERSON AND A HUMAN DOER.

MY LIFE BECAME PERFORMANCE BASED.

I DEVELOPED A SLAVE MENTALITY, NEVER FEELING FREE.

(ADD YOUR THOUGHTS ON HOW BELIEVING THIS LIE SHAPED YOUR THINKING)

____

____

____

____

I WANT TO REMOVE THESE LIES AND ASSOCIATED LIES FROM MY FOUNDATION RIGHT NOW.

(VISUALISE THE INCORRECT FOUNDATION BEING REMOVED).

I ASK FOR FORGIVENESS FOR THE WAYS I'VE HURT GOD, MYSELF AND OTHERS BY BELIEVING THIS LIE.

I NOW WANT TO REPLACE THE LIE WITH THE TRUTH AND THE TRUTH IS:

____

____

____

____

____

____

____

____

ATTENTION

I FORGIVE MYSELF FOR BELIEVING THE LIE THAT I WAS NOT WORTHY OF ATTENTION.

THIS MADE ME FEAR BEING IGNORED. IT ALSO CAUSED ME TO BE AN ATTENTION SEEKER AND TO FEEL THAT I HAD TO BECOME WHAT EVERYONE ELSE WANTED ME TO BE. I ALSO BELIEVED THAT WHAT I HAD TO SAY WAS NOT IMPORTANT AND THAT NOBODY CARED ABOUT ME.

MY LIFE BECAME PERFORMANCE BASED.

I DEVELOPED A SLAVE MENTALITY, NEVER FEELING FREE.

(ADD YOUR THOUGHTS ON HOW BELIEVING THIS LIE SHAPED YOUR THINKING)

____

____

____

____

I WANT TO REMOVE THESE LIES AND ASSOCIATED LIES FROM MY FOUNDATION RIGHT NOW.

(VISUALISE THE INCORRECT FOUNDATION BEING REMOVED).

I ASK FOR FORGIVENESS FOR THE WAYS I'VE HURT GOD, MYSELF AND OTHERS BY BELIEVING THIS LIE.

I NOW WANT TO REPLACE THE LIE WITH THE TRUTH AND THE TRUTH IS:

____

____

____

____

____

____

ENCOURAGEMENT

I FORGIVE MYSELF FOR BELIEVING THE LIE THAT I WAS NOT ENCOURAGED.

THIS MADE ME FEAR CRITICISM. IT ALSO CAUSED ME TO BECOME A PERFECTIONIST/PROCRASTINATOR. I BECAME NARROW IN MY THINKING, MAKING JUDGEMENTS AND ONLY SEEING THINGS IN TERMS OF 'BLACK AND WHITE'. I FELT FORCED TO FIGURE LIFE OUT FOR MYSELF, BECOMING INDEPENDENT AND SELF RELIANT.

MY LIFE BECAME PERFORMANCE BASED.

I DEVELOPED A SLAVE MENTALITY, NEVER FEELING FREE.

(ADD YOUR THOUGHTS ON HOW BELIEVING THIS LIE SHAPED YOUR THINKING)

____

____

____

____

I WANT TO REMOVE THOSE LIES AND ASSOCIATED LIES FROM MY FOUNDATION RIGHT NOW.

(VISUALISE THE INCORRECT FOUNDATION BEING REMOVED).

I ASK FOR FORGIVENESS FOR THE WAYS I'VE HURT GOD, MYSELF AND OTHERS BY BELIEVING THIS LIE.

I NOW WANT TO REPLACE THE LIE WITH THE TRUTH AND THE TRUTH IS:

____

____

____

____

____

____

RESPECT

I FORGIVE MYSELF FOR BELIEVING THE LIE THAT I WAS NOT RESPECTED OR VALUED.

THIS MADE ME FEAR WORTHLESSNESS. IT ALSO CAUSED ME TO DEVELOP A FALSE PERSONA AS I BELIEVED MY REAL SELF TO BE NOT GOOD ENOUGH. I BELIEVED I WASN'T WORTHY OF PRAISE AND SAW MYSELF AS DESERVING OF PUNISHMENT.

MY LIFE BECAME PERFORMANCE BASED.

I DEVELOPED A SLAVE MENTALITY, NEVER FEELING FREE.

(ADD YOUR THOUGHTS ON HOW BELIEVING THIS LIE SHAPED YOUR THINKING)

____

____

____

____

I WANT TO REMOVE THESE LIES AND ASSOCIATED LIES FROM MY FOUNDATION RIGHT NOW.

(VISUALISE THE INCORRECT FOUNDATION BEING REMOVED).

I ASK FOR FORGIVENESS FOR THE WAYS I'VE HURT GOD, MYSELF AND OTHERS BY BELIEVING THIS LIE.

I NOW WANT TO REPLACE THE LIE WITH THE TRUTH AND THE TRUTH IS:

____

____

____

____

____

APPENDIX THREE

emotional inventory

I. THE TOP 12 INTIMACY NEEDS

Here is a chart showing the top 12 intimacy needs that we all have:

Acceptance	accepting a person as they are, not trying to change them	
Affection	showing care and closeness through physical touch	
Affirmation	telling someone how great you think they are and pointing out their strengths	
Appreciation	showing gratefulness for someone through words and actions	
Approval	thinking and speaking well of someone	
Attention	conveying that you are listening to someone and interested in them	
Comfort (empathy)	coming alongside someone with word, touch and understanding	
Discipline	helping to bring order essential for healthy living into someone's life in a loving and caring manner	
Encouragement	urging someone forward and gently persuading them towards their goal	
Respect	valuing someone, regarding them highly, and conveying to them their worth	
Security	assurance of the permanence of a relationship and confidence of harmony in it	
Support	coming alongside someone and gently helping to carry a load	

II. EMOTIONAL INVENTORY QUESTIONNAIRE

This questionnaire will help an individual assess his or her most important intimacy needs. Answer the questions, then use the 'formula chart' to identify which needs you perceived as most important. If you like, have family members, friends, etc. complete the questionnaire and then discuss the results.

Instructions:

Respond to these questions by placing the appropriate number beside each sentence.

Strongly disagree	Disagree	Neutral	Agree	Strongly agree
-2	-1	0	+1	+2

1. It's important that people accept me for who I am – even if I'm a little 'different' ☐
2. It's very important to me that my financial world is in order ☐
3. I sometimes become 'fed up of doing what is right' ☐
4. It's vital to me that others ask me my opinion ☐
5. It's important that I receive frequent physical hugs, warm embraces, etc. ☐
6. I feel especially good when someone 'knows me' ☐
7. It's important for me to know 'where I stand' with those who are in authority over me ☐
8. It is particularly meaningful when someone notices that I need help and then they offer to get involved ☐
9. If I feel overwhelmed, I especially want someone to come alongside me and help ☐

10. I feel important when someone recognises and shows concern for how I'm feeling emotionally ☐
11. I always like to know if 'who I am' is of value and is meaningful to others ☐
12. Generally speaking, I don't like a lot of solitude ☐
13. It means a lot to me for loved ones to initiate an 'I love you' ☐
14. I resist being seen only as a part of a large group – my individuality is important ☐
15. I am particularly pleased when a friend calls to listen and encourage me ☐
16. It's important to me that people acknowledge me not just for what I do but for who I am ☐
17. I feel best when my world is orderly and somewhat predictable ☐
18. When I've worked hard on a project, I am pleased to have people acknowledge my work and express gratitude ☐
19. When I 'blow it', it's especially important to me to be reassured that I'm still loved ☐
20. It's particularly encouraging to me when I realise that others notices my positive qualities ☐
21. I sometimes feel overwhelmed and discouraged ☐
22. I want to be treated with kindness and equality by all regardless of my race, gender, looks, status ☐
23. The sexual aspect of relationships is/would be very important to me ☐
24. I love it when someone wants to spend time with just me ☐

25. I am particularly pleased when a 'superior' says, 'Well done' ☐
26. It's very important to me for someone to hold me and love me after I've had a hard day ☐
27. While I feel confident about what I do' (my talents, gifts, etc.) I always sense that I need other people's input and help ☐
28. Written notes and calls expressing sympathy after the death of a loved one, health problems, divorce are very meaningful to me ☐
29. I feel good when someone close to me shows satisfaction with the way I am ☐
30. I enjoy being spoken of or mentioned in front of a group of people ☐
31. I would be described as a 'touchy/feely' person ☐
32. When a decision is going to affect my life, It's important to me that I have a 'say so in the decision ☐
33. I am particularly pleased when someone shows interest in current projects I'm working on ☐
34. I appreciate trophies, plaques and special gifts which are a permanent reminder of something significant which I have done ☐
35. I sometimes worry about the future ☐
36. When I'm introduced into a new environment, I immediately search for a group of people to connect with ☐
37. The thought of change (moving, new job. etc) produces anxiety for me ☐

38. It bothers me when people are prejudiced against someone just because they dress or act differently ☐
39. It's necessary to me to be surrounded by friends and loved ones who will be there 'through thick and thin' ☐
40. I am particularly pleased by written notes and phrases of gratitude ☐
41. To know that someone is constantly praying for me is very meaningful ☐
42. I am particularly bothered by 'controlling' people ☐
43. I am particularly pleased by unmerited and spontaneous expressions of love ☐
44. I am pleased when someone looks me in the eye and listens to me speak ☐
45. I am particularly pleased when people commend me for a godly characteristic I exhibit ☐
46. I never want to be alone when experiencing hurt and trouble; it's important for me to have someone with me ☐
47. I really don't enjoy working on a project by myself; I prefer to have a partner on every project ☐
48. It's important for me to feel a 'part of the group' ☐
49. I really respond to someone who tries to understand me emotionally and who shows me loving concern ☐
50. When working on a project, I would much rather work with a team of people than by myself ☐

1. Add up your responses (-2, -1, 0, +1, +2) to items

   1 ________________

   19________________

   36________________

   38________________

   48________________

Total: ________________

These responses relate to the need for ACCEPTANCE

2. Add up your responses to items:

   2 ________________

   17________________

   35________________

   37________________

   39________________

Total: ________________

These responses relate to the need for SECURITY

3. Add up your responses to items:

   16________________

   18________________

   20________________

   34________________

   40________________

Total: ________________

These responses relate to the need for APPRECIATION

4. Add up your responses to items:

   3 ________________

   15________________

   21________________

   33________________

   41________________

Total: ________________

These responses relate to the needs for ENCOURAGEMENT

5. Add up your responses to items:

   4 ________________

   14________________

   22________________

   32________________

   42________________

Total: ________________

These responses relate to the need for RESPECT

6. Add up your responses to items:

   5 ________________

   13________________

   23________________

   31________________

   43________________

Total: ________________

These responses relate to the need for AFFECTION

7. Add up your responses to items:

6 ________________

12________________

24________________

30________________

44________________

Total: ________________

These responses relate to the need for ATTENTION

8. Add up your responses to items:

7 ________________

11________________

25________________

29________________

45________________

Total: ________________

These responses relate to the need for APPROVAL

9. Add up your responses to items:

10________________

26________________

28________________

46________________

49________________

Total: ________________

These responses relate to the need for COMFORT

10.Add up your responses to items:

8 ________________

9 ________________

27________________

47________________

50________________

Total: ________________

These responses relate to the need for SUPPORT

Reflect on/discuss the following:

1. What were your three highest totals? Which needs do they represent?
2. What were your three lowest total? Which needs do they represent?
3. If there are others completing this questionnaire with you (friend, spouse, other family members, etc.) what were their highest and lowest totals?
4. What might be the implications of your scores compared to their scores?

III. CURRENT NEEDS AND CHILDHOOD NEEDS:

The Potential and The Pain

1. Look at the three needs you selected as most important to you. How do you **feel** when your spouse **meets** one or more of these needs?

____

____

____

   What **thoughts** go through your mind?

____

____

____

   How do you **act?**

____

____

____

2. What **feelings** do you have when these needs go **unmet**?

____

____

____

   What **thoughts** go through your mind?

____

____

____

   How do you **act?**

____

____

____

3. When I think back over my childhood, I especially remember **needing** ____________________________________
______________________________ from my mother.

Was there ever a time when it was important for your mother to meet these needs and she did not? If so, write about it here:

____

____

____

4. When I think about my childhood, I remember especially **needing** ____
____ from my father.

Was there ever a time when it was important for your father to meet these needs, and he did not? If so, write about it here:

____

____

____

5. When these needs went **unmet** in my childhood, I remember **thinking**

____

____

____

I remember d**oing**

____

____

____

____

6. Did your family tend to **deny or ignore** your needs?
Yes ______ No______

Elaborate on your answer here:

____

____

____

7. Did your family tend to **blame or criticise** you in response to your needs?
Yes ______ No______

Elaborate on your answer here:

8. What three **needs** from the 'Top 12' list do you think you **missed most** during your childhood? Write about this here:

9. Now compare the three needs you would most like to have met by your partner with either the three needs you **missed most** from your childhood, or with needs that were **consistently and abundantly met.** Are there any **similarities or correlations?** Explain:

references further reading

Biddulph, Steve (1984) *The Secret of Happy Children.* Sydney: Bay Books.

Breggin, Peter R., M.D. *Talking Back To Ritalin.* Cambridge, MA: Perseus Publishing.

Clare, Anthony (2000) *On Men: Masculinity In Crisis.* London: Chatto & Windus.

Cohen, David (2001) *The Father's Book: Being A Good Dad In The 21st Century.* Chicester: John Wiley & Sons, Ltd.

Ehrensaft, Diane, Ph.D. (1997) *Spoiling Childhood: How Well-Meaning Parents Are Giving Children Too Much – But Not What They Need.* New York: The Guilford Press.

Eldredge, John (2001) *Wild At Heart: Discovering The Secret Of A Man's Soul.* Nashville: Thomas Nelson Publishers.

Ferguson, Dr. David, Teresa Ferguson, Dr. Paul Warren, Vicky Warren and Terri Ferguson (1995) *Parenting With Intimacy.* Wheaton, Illinois: Victor Books.

Ferguson, Dr. David, Teresa Ferguson, Dr. Paul Warren, Vicky Warren and Terri Ferguson (1995) *Parenting With Intimacy Workbook.* Wheaton, Illinois: Victor Books.

Frank, Robert Ph.D. with Kathryn E. Livingston (2002) *The Secret Life of the Dyslexic Child.* New York: Rodale/St. Martin's Press.

Greene, Sheila (2003) *The Psychological Development of Girls and Women.* East Sussex: Routledge.

Gurian, Michael (1994) *Mothers, Sons & Lovers: How A Man's Relationship with His Mother Affects the Rest of His Life.* Boston: Shambhala Publications, Inc.

Gurian, Michael (1999) *The Good Son: Shaping The Moral Development of Our Boys and Young Men.* New York: Jeremy P. Tarcher / Putnam.

Gurian, Michael (2003) *What Could He Be Thinking?: How A Man's Mind Really Works.* New York: St. Martin's Press.

Hemfelt, Dr. Robert and Dr. Paul Warren (1990) *Kids Who Carry Our Pain.* Nashville: Thomas Nelson Publishers.

Jacobs, Gregg D. Ph.D. *The Ancestral Mind.* New York: Viking.

Lang, Gregory E. (2002) *Why a Daughter Needs a Dad: 100 Reasons* (with photographs by Janet Lankford-Moran). Nashville: Cumberland House Publishing, Inc.

Lang, Gregory E. (2003) *Why a Son Needs a Dad: 100 Reasons* (with photographs by Janet Lankford-Moran). Nashville: Cumberland House Publishing, Inc.

Mamen, Maggie (2004) *The Pampered Child Syndrome.* Ottowa: Creative Bound International, Inc.

Parsons, Rob (1995) *The Sixty Minute Father: An Hour To Change Your Child's Life.* London: Hodder & Stoughton.

Pollack, William S, Ph.D and Kathleen Cushman (2001) *Real Boys Workbook.* New York: Villard Books.

Power, Louis, ed. (2000) *Parenting In The Millenium: Birth to Twelve.* Booterstown, Co. Dublin: Nurture Press, including "Parent/Child Intimacy" by Owen Connolly (p.17-23).

Seligman, Martin E.P., Ph.D. (1993) *What You Can Change and What You Can't: Learning To Accept Who You Are.* New York: Fawcett Columbine.

Shaw, Robert, M.D. with Stephanie Wood (2003) *The Epidemic: The Rot of American Culture, Absentee and Permissive Parenting, and the Resultant Plague of Joyless, Selfish Children.* New York: HarperCollins Publishers Inc.

Skelton, Christine (2001) Schooling The Boys: Masculinities and Primary Education. Buckingham: Open University Press.

Stabiner, Karen (2002) *All Girls: Single-Sex Education and Why It Matters.* New York: Riverhead Books.

Wallerstein, Judith S. and Sandra Blakeslee (1995) *The Good Marriage: How and Why Love Lasts.* Boston: Houghton Mifflin Company.

"STANDING ON THE SHOULDERS OF GIANTS" SEMINARS

Owen Connolly and The Nurture Institute run day-long seminars on fatherhood called "Standing On the Shoulders of Giants." Here's what some fathers had to say about how they benefited from this course…

Now I'm able to…

- consider my children's comments and actions differently
- think more cleverly about my role as a father
- talk openly to my four kids
- better address personal issues related to my family of origin and my own family
- improve the way I interact with my children
- understand my children's problems better and appreciate their world as well as my own
- think about treating my children and grandparents in a different way
- look for and listen to what people are actually saying
- look at my parental role in a less defensive way and be a little more relaxed and enjoy the father role rather than just feeling pressure and responsibility
- be more prepared to listen to what my children are saying rather than assuming I know what they want to say
- understand and accept my kids a little better
- appreciate how much deeper parenting is and to realise developmental differences between boys and girls
- better perceive emotional demands and listen

Now I know...

- That my role as a father is very important
- My parents only passed on what they had
- I can change and improve for the better
- That children react emotionally up to a certain age... I must try to remember that when conflict arises
- Parenting each child is unique
- My relationship with my wife if very important to me and my boys need to see Father loves Mummy
- More ways in which my own childhood experiences translate into aspects of my relationship with my children
- I have to treat my children differently and be a better father
- That encouragement, attention, and acceptance are really important for the healthy development of my children
- There's a lot more to parenting than meets the eye
- I need to play more with my child

Now I feel...

- More confident as a father
- I can do better
- Hopeful, aware, confident, blessed, and there's work to be done
- I will be able to talk to my spouse and kids openly and honestly for the first time ever
- A little more secure in my role as father
- Less isolated in my parental role
- More confident in my capacity to improve as a parent and overcome some of the difficulties I have had

- I have something to contribute to my child
- A little happier about how I've been performing as a parent
- Better able to pro-actively approach my son with some of the challenges I faced
- I understand how my own upbringing has affected my dealings with my daughter

Now I have decided...

- Praise, thank, and talk more with all the family
- To take a more active role as a father
- To start loving myself unconditionally and my children also
- To try and improve as a father and person
- To share some of the things I have learned today with my spouse. Working together should make things easier
- To discuss and try ways and means of reforming my ways to the benefit of my kids
- To read further
- To be aware of my children's growth, development, and needs
- To improve my relationship with my wife for us as a family at present and for the boys in the future
- To try to find ways to address my own needs without guilt or feeling inadequate for having to ask or state explicitly that I have needs
- To talk with other fathers about our role
- To keep at it in terms of exploring new ways of experiencing my childrens' childhood

- To enjoy and love my kids without judging or having preconceived ideas of how they should be
- To spend more time with my children
- To put more time, attention, and listening into my family
- To pay attention to what my children are trying to communicate, as opposed to trying to mould the way they should think
- To try and implement the idea of giving choices instead of doing things instantaneously.

For information on when and where these seminars are held, see www.nurture.ie